The
Woman
Entrepreneur

The
Woman
Entrepreneur

---

*Starting, Financing,
and Managing a
Successful New Business*

Robert D. Hisrich

AND

Candida G. Brush

Lexington Books

D.C. Heath and Company/Lexington, Massachusetts/Toronto

Library of Congress Cataloging in Publication Data

Hisrich, Robert D.
The woman entrepreneur.

Includes index.
1. New business enterprises—Management.
2. Women-owned business enterprises—Management.
I. Brush, Candida G. II. Title.
HD62.5.H58   1985   658.4′ 2   84–48256
ISBN 0-669-09189-8 (alk. paper)

Second Printing, April 1986
Published simultaneously in Canada
Printed in the United States of America
International Standard Book Number: 0-669-09189-8
Library of Congress Catalog Card Number: 84-48256

The paper used in this publication meets the minimum requirements of
American National Standard for Information Sciences—Permanence
of Paper for Printed Library Materials, ANSI Z39.48-1984.
∞TM

Dedicated to our daughters,
Emily, Juliette, Kary, Katy, Kelly, and Lucy,
women entrepreneurs of the future

Contents

Figures

Tables

Preface

Starting and operating a business entails considerable risk and effort. In creating and building a business, the entrepreneur assumes all the responsibilities for its development and management, as well as for the corresponding risks and rewards. The increased interest in this activity can be seen in the increasing research on the subject, the increased number of college courses on entrepreneurship, and the more than two million new enterprises started each year despite a 70 percent failure rate.

The risk of failure in starting a new enterprise is perhaps even greater for the woman entrepreneur, who in addition to all the usual business problems must deal with the problem of being a woman in a traditionally male-dominated arena. Who is this woman entrepreneur? She may be a nurse, a student, a teacher, a homemaker, a manager, or any woman in a position that does not bring her fulfillment. She is a person who is willing to juggle her life between work and family, between a career and marriage. She is caught by family responsibilities on the one hand and career responsibilities on the other. The woman entrepreneur may find, for example, that getting help with household chores from a husband is not easy and that hiring a responsible caretaker for young children can be expensive. But, in spite of the obstacles, the number of women entrepreneurs is increasing at three times the rate of men. This growth in the number of women entrepreneurs and the additional 85 percent of all women who say they would like to be in business for themselves prompted the writing of this book.

The book is divided into two overall sections: the first two chapters describe the background and characteristics of women entrepreneurs, and chapters 3–7 discuss the various factors involved in starting and managing a new enterprise. The book should be of interest to those women who have succeeded as entrepreneurs and are now managing their enterprise, to women who are in some stage of developing the enterprise, and to women who are considering starting their own businesses. By describing the characteristics of the entrepreneur and the business side of entrepreneurship, this book gives help to the new entrepreneurial woman who is either reentering the business world or is considering a career change, and to those women entrepreneurs who are experiencing some of the problems mentioned here. Through discussion of the experiences, problems, and successes of women entrepreneurs, the book gives needed advice and encouragement to present and future women entrepreneurs of all kinds.

Our book is based on a major research project whereby over 1,000 women entrepreneurs across the nation were surveyed by mail questionnaire. The 41 percent (468) women entrepreneurs who responded provided us with valuable data which serve as a foundation for this effort. In addition, 35 women entrepreneurs were selected from the above group to be further queried in personal and telephone interviews. We are grateful for the interest, assistance, and openness of all the women entrepreneurs who participated in our research.

Many people have helped to make this book possible: the many women entrepreneurs who spent hours sharing their experiences and needs with us, as well as commenting on various parts of the manuscript; Georgina Wolf, who typed the manuscript; Daphanne Mowatt, who provided research material and editorial assistance; Barra O'Cinneide, Dean, National Institute for Higher Education, Limerick, Ireland, and Robert Monroe, Dean, University of Tulsa, who gave us advice and encouragement; and Bruce Katz, who made helpful editorial comments. We are deeply indebted to our spouses, Tina and David, and to our children, Emily, Juliette, Kary, Katy, Kelly, and Lucy, whose patience, support, encouragement, and love helped bring this effort to fruition. It is to these future women entrepreneurs—Emily, Juliette, Kary, Katy, Kelly, and Lucy—that this book is particularly dedicated.

1
A Historical Perspective

When people ask me if I like being in business, I usually respond: on days when there are more sales than problems, I love it; on days when there are more problems than sales, I wonder why I do it. Basically, I am in business because it gives me a good feeling about myself. You learn a lot about your capabilities by putting yourself on the line. Running a successful business is not only a financial risk; it is an emotional risk as well. I get a lot of satisfaction from having dared it—done it—and been successful.

Does this quote from a woman entrepreneur fit your picture of what it's like to be an entrepreneur? It says a lot about what it takes to start and operate a successful business. The risks are indeed there, as they were for Karen Stein, who left her position as a leading designer for a major comforter, pillow, and curtain manufacturer in New York to start the Karen Stein Collection. As founder, president, and designer, Ms. Stein expanded her company to include a line of over three hundred accessories and girls' clothing items, employing twenty-four women in manufacturing, all in just 2½ years. The company has achieved national recognition for its distinctive ribbon designs in hearts, penguins, plaids, polka dots, rainbows, stripes, and watermelons. These and other products in the line are sold in boutiques, department stores, and specialty shops throughout the United States. The company's rapid growth and success will continue thanks to the design originality of its founder, Karen Stein.

Karen Stein is not alone. More and more women are starting their own businesses in a variety of fields, some of which have traditionally been dominated by men. The idea of being an entrepreneur is certainly appealing. But what is an entrepreneur and how do you know if entrepreneurship is for you?

What Does It Mean to Be an Entrepreneur?

Who is an entrepreneur? What is entrepreneurship? These questions are frequently asked by those interested in entrepreneurship. The term itself—*entrepreneur*—comes from the French and literally translated means "between-taker" or "go-between."

An early example of a "go-between" is Marco Polo. He attempted to establish trade routes to the Far East, and as was the custom, he signed a contract in advance to sell a manufacturer's goods. The common contract of the times included a loan from an investor to a merchant adventurer making the investor a passive risk-bearer and the merchant adventurer an active bearer of the physical risks. Upon the successful completion of a journey by a merchant adventurer, the capitalist, not the entrepreneur, took the majority of the profits.

In the Middle Ages the term *entrepreneur* was used to describe someone who managed large production projects. This kind of entrepreneur would not take any risks himself, but would manage the project using the resources provided. For example, the person overseeing the construction of great architectural works, like castles and fortifications, public buildings, abbeys, and cathedrals, was seen as an entrepreneur.

The concept of the risk involved in entrepreneurship changed somewhat by the seventeenth century, when the entrepreneur came to be seen as someone who entered into a contractual arrangement with the government either to perform a service or to supply certain products. Any resulting profits (or losses) were the result of the entrepreneur's efforts, since the contract price was fixed. For example, John Law received permission from a French prince regent to establish a royal bank, and from this enterprise evolved an exclusive franchise to form a trading company in the New World, the Mississippi Company. One of Law's contemporaries, the author Richard Cantillon, developed one of the early theories of the entrepreneur as a risk-taker. He noted that merchants, farmers, craftsmen, and other sole proprietors "buy at a certain price and sell at an uncertain price, therefore operating at a risk."[1]

By the eighteenth century, the entrepreneur with capital was distinguished from one needing capital. In other words, the entrepreneurial role was distinguished from a capital-providing role.

In the nineteenth century entrepreneurs were seldom distinguished from managers and were mainly viewed from an economic perspective, not from the perspective of creating something new. Andrew Carnegie is probably the best example of a nineteenth-century entrepreneur in that he invented nothing, but adapted and introduced new technology and products into economic life.

Finally, in the twentieth century the entrepreneur came to be seen as an innovator. Joseph Schumpeter put it this way:

> The function of entrepreneurs is to reform or revolutionize the pattern of production by exploiting an invention or, more generally, an untried technological possibility for producing a new commodity or producing an old one in a new way, opening a new source of supply of materials or a new outlet for products, by reorganizing a new industry . . . [2]

Innovation and newness are both integral parts of entrepreneurship in this definition. Newness could mean anything from a new product to a new distribution system to simply a new organizational structure. Edward Harriman, who reorganized the Ontario and Southern Railways through the Northern Pacific Trust, or John Pierpont Morgan, who developed his large banking house by reorganizing and financing the nation's industries, were entrepreneurs in this sense.

Our portrait of the entrepreneur can be further developed through business, managerial, and personal perspectives, which give us some of the more recent definitions:

> To an economist, an entrepreneur is one who brings resources, labor, materials, and other assets into combinations that make their value greater than before, and also one who introduces changes, innovations, and a new order. To a psychologist, such a person is typically driven by certain forces—need to obtain or attain something, to experiment, to accomplish, or perhaps to escape authority of others . . . To one businessman, an entrepreneur appears as a threat, an aggressive competitor, whereas to

another businessman the same entrepreneur may be an ally, a
source of supply, a customer, or someone good to invest in. . . .
The same person is seen by a capitalist philosopher as one who
creates wealth for others as well, who finds better ways to utilize
resources, and reduce waste, and who produces jobs others are
glad to get.[3]

Each of these characterizations develops from a slightly different
perspective, yet each contains some similar notions: newness, organization, creation of wealth, and risk-taking. Finally, though, each
characterization is somewhat simplistic. Entrepreneurs are found in
all professions—teaching, medicine, research, law, architecture,
engineering, social work, and business. Therefore, to account for all
types of entrepreneurial behavior, we give the following definition:
Entrepreneurship is the process of creating something different of
value by devoting the necessary time and effort, by assuming the accompanying financial, psychological, and social risks, and by receiving the resulting rewards of monetary and personal satisfaction. For
the person actually starting a business, the experience is filled with
enthusiasm, frustration, anxiety, and hard work. Businesses characteristically have a higher failure rate because of poor sales, intense
competition, or lack of capital. The risks, both financial and emotional, can be very high.

For the woman entrepreneur, the risk is even greater. She has
the additional problems of working in a male-dominated arena,
having few role models, and lacking confidence in her business
skills. According to one woman entrepreneur,

> The biggest roadblocks to women's success are their lack of ex-
> perience and thus undeveloped business-related skills, such as in-
> dependence, self-confidence, assertiveness, and drive (skills men
> learn growing up), and the relative absence of a defined women's
> network for business referrals, which act as inroads to other suc-
> cessful businesses.

Are You an Entrepreneur?

Before we consider the various demographic, sociological, and psychological characteristics of the typical woman entrepreneur (which

are discussed throughout the first three chapters), let us make clear that a woman considering entrepreneurship as a career path should not be alarmed if she does not possess all the characteristics. As a potential woman entrepreneur, you may be a secretary, nurse, teacher, homemaker, or manager. To become an entrepreneur, though, you have to make two decisions. First, you have to decide to change your present career and lifestyle. This decision may be made for you if you are fired or move because of your spouse's new position. You may be motivated to make this decision by job frustration or by lack of advancement opportunity, or you may have recognized a market opportunity.

The second decision you must make is to determine that an entrepreneurial career is both attractive and feasible for you. This decision involves assessment of personal feelings on control, independence, and risk.[4]

A common concern among women considering an entrepreneurial venture is whether they will be able to sustain enough drive and energy to create and manage a new enterprise. Are you driven by an inner need to succeed and win? You can make an initial assessment by using the checklist in figure 1–1. After answering the questions, compare your answers with those at the end of this chapter to see whether you are the kind of person who is motivated from the inside—a characteristic of most women entrepreneurs.

Closely related to this feeling of control is the need for independence. A potential woman entrepreneur should consider whether she is the kind of person who needs to do things in her job in her own way and time. Answer the checklist in figure 1–2 and compare your answers with those at the end of the chapter to see if you have a strong need for independence, another characteristic of most women entrepreneurs.

To acquire independence, you must be willing to undertake a certain amount of risk. Each potential woman entrepreneur should assess her risk-taking behavior by answering the questions in figure 1–3. From a comparison with the answers at the end of the chapter you can determine whether or not you are a risk-taker.

While you need not check out as a completely inner-directed, totally independent risk-taker to be a potential entrepreneur, you should be aware of your own characteristics before you decide on

1. Do you often feel "That's just the way things are and there's nothing I can do about it"? ____ Yes ____ No

2. When things go right and are terrific for you, do you think "It's mostly luck!"? ____ Yes ____ No

3. Do you think you "should" go into business or do something with your time for pay because everything you read these days is urging you in that direction? ____ Yes ____ No

4. Do you know that if you decide to do something, you'll do it and nothing can stop you? ____ Yes ____ No

5. Even though it's scary to try something new, are you the kind who tries it? ____ Yes ____ No

6. Your friends, husband, and mother tell you that it's foolish of you to want a career. Have you listened to them and stayed home all these years? ____ Yes ____ No

7. Do you think it's important for everyone to like you? ____ Yes ____ No

8. When you do a good job, is your pleasure in a job well-done satisfaction enough? ____ Yes ____ No

9. If you want something, do you ask for it rather than wait for someone to notice you and "just give it to you"? ____ Yes ____ No

10. Even though people tell you "it can't be done," do you have to find out for yourself? ____ Yes ____ No

Source: Sandra Winston, *The Entrepreneurial Woman* (New York: Newsweek Books, 1979), 31–32.

Figure 1–1. *Checklist for Feelings on Control*

an entrepreneurial career. These issues are discussed in greater detail in chapter 3.

Women in the Work Force, Then and Now

The role of women in the workplace has undergone a change in the last forty-five years. Forty-five years ago only a small minority of women owned and operated their own businesses. In fact, in 1940 women made up less than 26 percent of the entire American work force, with most of those women employed as nurses, secretaries, or teachers. World War II brought many more women into the work force, but a man was still considered the head of the household and

1. I hate to go shopping for clothes alone.	____ Yes	____ No
2. If my friends won't go to a movie I want to see, I'll go by myself.	____ Yes	____ No
3. I want to be financially independent.	____ Yes	____ No
4. I often need to ask other people's opinions before I decide on important things.	____ Yes	____ No
5. I'd rather have other people decide where to go on a social evening out.	____ Yes	____ No
6. When I know I'm in charge, I don't apologize, I just do what has to be done.	____ Yes	____ No
7. I'll speak up for an unpopular cause if I believe in it.	____ Yes	____ No
8. I'm afraid to be different.	____ Yes	____ No
9. I want the approval of others.	____ Yes	____ No
10. I usually wait for people to call me to go places, rather than intrude on them.	____ Yes	____ No

Source: Sandra Winston, *The Entrepreneurial Woman* (New York: Newsweek Books, 1979), 34–35.

Figure 1–2. *Checklist for Feelings on Independence*

1. Can you take risks with money, that is, invest, and not know the outcome?	____ Yes	____ No
2. Do you take an umbrella with you every time you travel? A hot water bottle? A thermometer?	____ Yes	____ No
3. If you're frightened of something, will you try to conquer the fear?	____ Yes	____ No
4. Do you like trying new food, new places, and totally new experiences?	____ Yes	____ No
5. Do you need to know the answer before you'll ask the question?	____ Yes	____ No
6. Have you taken a risk in the last six months?	____ Yes	____ No
7. Can you walk up to a total stranger and strike up a conversation?	____ Yes	____ No
8. Have you ever intentionally travelled on an unfamiliar route?	____ Yes	____ No
9. Do you need to know that it's been done already before you're willing to try it?	____ Yes	____ No
10. Have you ever gone on a blind date?	____ Yes	____ No

Source: Sandra Winston, *The Entrepreneurial Woman* (New York: Newsweek Books, 1979), 42.

Figure 1–3. *Checklist for Willingness to Take Risks*

women remained independent by staying home to raise the children. In other words, the changes brought about by World War II did not motivate women to work outside the home unless it was necessary. There was even less motivation for women to start their own businesses. If a woman worked at all, her job was usually secondary to her husband's or to jobs of men in general, and was often part-time where lower wages were earned.

But even since the turn of the century, women have tried to overcome some of the barriers imposed by these accepted social roles. Charlotte Perkins Gilman, a noted writer, stated in *Women and Economics* in the early 1900s that women's oppression was rooted in their roles as wives and mothers. She argued that women needed to work outside the home to be independent and called for large housing units where child care, cooking, and cleaning would be done by professionals.[5]

In certain fields, women have generally been more accepted as business owners. Frequently, beauty parlors, nursery schools, and some retail establishments, like those selling women's apparel, children's clothing, or crafts, were owned by women. However, preconceived notions of a woman's "rightful place" or innate talents have created occupational stereotypes and have limited opportunities for women in certain areas, like finance, manufacturing, and research and development. Unfortunately, these stereotypes not only have limited a woman's ability to gain needed management experience, but also have created obstacles for women business owners trying to establish credibility in such areas such as banking, construction, or engineering.

In the past twenty-five years, significant social, political, and economic changes have created opportunities for women and given them greater acceptance in the business world. Many things have affected working women: the desire of college students of the 1960s and 1970s to "find themselves"; the focus on the "me generation"; women's liberation; and subsequent legislation prohibiting sex discrimination. Bureau of Labor statistics indicate over 50 percent of the adult women in the United States now hold jobs outside the home, and that figure is growing. More and more women are studying business, law, engineering, and computer science, which means that more women will have the skills and confidence necessary for establishing their own businesses. In addition, social trends, such as an increasing number of divorces, an increasing number of single parent families, later marriages, postponement of child rearing, and partnership marriages, have dramatically changed society's perception of women, a change that has had enormous impact in the world of business. It is now more acceptable for women to work and have a family, or to have a career and not be married, or to work in a field traditionally dominated by men, like construction, commercial aviation, or medicine. Generally, women now have more independence and confidence to venture out alone than ever before. Of course the path to self-employment has obstacles.

Claudia Tischler, of Quadra Construction in St. Paul, Minnesota, is an example of a woman who has successfully entered a male-dominated field:

> As a woman in a traditional business of men, I have found a lack of belief that a woman can operate a construction firm—men are sure that if you can't pound a nail, then you know zip about construction. I constantly have to prove my company's ability with oversell and by cutting prices to get in the door with a client.

Her difficulties in establishing credibility notwithstanding, Ms. Tischler has made her business a success; she employs more than fifty people and grosses over $1 million annually.

Women Entrepreneurs Today

In spite of the obstacles and risks, an increasing number of women have decided in the past decade to start their own businesses. The Bureau of Census issued a report using 1972 data showing that women-owned businesses accounted for only 4.6 percent of all firms in the United States, with the receipts from women-owned businesses making up only .03 percent of all business receipts in the United States. According to a more recent Bureau of Labor report, self-employment among women experienced five times the growth rate of self-employment among men between 1972 and 1979. According to another study by the Small Business Administration, the level of self-employment for women increased from 1.5 million in 1972 to 2.1 million in 1979, and to approximately 2.3 million in

Table 1–1

Percentage of Women-owned Businesses by State

State	Percentage
Alabama	20.4%
Alaska	19.6%
Arizona	25.6%
Arkansas	15.4%
California	27.7%
Colorado	24.1%
Connecticut	25.1%
Delaware	23.5%
District of Columbia	32.5%
Florida	24.4%
Georgia	20.5%
Hawaii	32.5%
Idaho	17.3%
Illinois	25.5%
Indiana	22.5%
Iowa	18.5%
Kansas	19.9%
Kentucky	16.8%
Louisiana	17.9%
Maine	20.7%
Maryland	27.4%
Massachusetts	22.2%
Michigan	21.0%
Minnesota	20.7%
Mississippi	19.2%
Missouri	17.2%
Montana	25.1%
Nebraska	18.1%
Nevada	27.4%
New Hampshire	24.8%
New Jersey	22.3%
New Mexico	22.2%
New York	23.3%
North Carolina	20.4%
North Dakota	16.8%
Ohio	23.8%
Oklahoma	17.3%
Oregon	20.6%
Pennsylvania	20.4%
Rhode Island	21.0%
South Carolina	25.4%
South Dakota	15.5%
Tennessee	16.9%
Texas	18.2%

Table 1–1 continued

State	Percentage
Utah	21.4%
Vermont	24.6%
Virginia	24.9%
Washington	24.6%
West Virginia	25.1%
Wisconsin	20.0%
Wyoming	23.8%

Source: South Middlesex News, March 7, 1982, p. 10.

1981. More recent statistics put the number of self-employed women at 3.5 million in 1984. While the percentage of businesses started and operated by women in the United States is small, with estimates ranging from 4.6 percent to 5.7 percent, the absolute number of women-owned enterprises is impressively large.

The number of businesses owned and operated by women varies from state to state. A study by the Small Business Administration found that women-owned businesses were more prevalent in California, Hawaii, Ohio, Illinois, and in states along the East Coast, and were less prevalent in Arkansas, South Dakota, Kentucky, and North Dakota. A state-by-state breakdown of women-owned firms appears in table 1–1.

Today, women have a greater role in the work force, increasingly as business owners. Let us now examine the basic characteristics of the businesses that women are starting today and take a closer look at the women themselves.

Perhaps most significant is that most of the businesses started by women are less than five years old. Only about 30 percent of all female-owned businesses have been operating for more than five years. The newness of these businesses partly explains the markedly low average gross revenues (less than $500,000 annually) of the majority of women-owned businesses. Since it usually takes two to three years before any business starts to turn a profit, revenues are likely to increase significantly as the businesses continue to grow and mature. Second, the youth of these businesses coincides with recent strong economic trends and with the return to entrepreneurship in recent years; aside from the recession in 1980–1981, these years have provided great opportunities for new business start-ups.

Another characteristic of women-owned businesses is the nature
of the business endeavor. Based on our research, over 90 percent of
the businesses begun by women are service related; the figures for
manufacturing and finance are only 7 percent and 3 percent respectively. These percentages are consistent, however, with percentages
in the overall economy, which is heavily service-oriented and in
which less than 25 percent of all businesses are found in manufacturing. But, more women are starting businesses in high technology
areas, such as software production or computer services, where
there are considerable growth opportunities. This means that
women are being perceptive in moving toward growing fields.

The business ventures of women entrepreneurs range from inno-
vative (a private post office) to typically male-dominated areas (petroleum products and plumbing installation) to traditional service-
related areas (travel agencies and clothing stores). Most businesses
are in the areas of educational services, retail sales, consulting, and
public relations (see table 1–2). In these businesses, the innovation is
an improved or new service, which indicates the women entrepreneurs' ability to assess market needs and to determine a niche. Real
innovation is an important asset in a new enterprise from a competitive and profit standpoint. It is usually the dynamic new inventions
or product/service modifications that have the opportunity for significant growth and profit.

The high number of service-oriented businesses owned by
women also reflects the educational and occupational background

Table 1–2
Nature of Businesses Started
by Women Entrepreneurs

Type of Business	Percentage of Women Polled
Retail sales	7.6%
Consulting	7.6%
Educational services	4.1%
Public relations	3.9%
Career consulting	3.9%
Personal services	3.7%
Word processing	3.5%
Real estate	3.5%
Advertising	3.2%

of many women entrepreneurs. Most women have had a liberal arts college education and a service-related occupational experience. This typical background reflects the values that at one time defined socially acceptable occupations for women and is a result of the advice of guidance counselors who discouraged women from entering male-dominated fields. You can easily see how the liberal arts/service background creates obstacles for the woman seeking to start a manufacturing concern. Several women entrepreneurs commented on the need to raise society's expectations for the female population and the necessity for better career guidance and advice for women students.

The service orientation of the businesses started by women also affects the size of the business in terms of number of employees; the average business employs fewer than five. This is not unusual because most service businesses are not labor-intensive.

Eunice Dorholts's business is fairly typical. Her flower shop, Country Sunshine, represents her third entrepreneurial venture. She is single and has two sons, one teenage and one college age. Her education was in the humanities, and her occupational experience included management/secretarial work. Her business is less than five years old and employs three to five part-time employees; annual revenues are under the $500,000 mark. Although the idea of a flower shop is not unique, Ms. Dorholts's business offers some unique arrangements not only in fresh flowers, but also in silk and other artificial flowers. Her advice to future entrepreneurs is:

> Be in touch with realism. Learn about business skills through education or experts. In my business it's easy to get caught up in the creative aspects, but it still comes down to making money.

Female and Male Entrepreneurs

Even though there has been significant growth in female self-employment, most of what is known about the characteristics of entrepreneurs, their motivations, backgrounds, families, educational and occupational experiences, and problems, is based on studies of male entrepreneurs. This is not surprising since men make up the majority of people who start and own their own businesses. Interest in women entrepreneurs is a more recent phenomenon.

Studies of female entrepreneurs have addressed basically the same questions as those of male entrepreneurs. One study of twenty female entrepreneurs found that their prime motivations for starting a business were: the need to achieve, the desire to be independent, the need for job satisfaction, and economic necessity. These female entrepreneurs tended to have an autocratic style of management, and their major problem during start-up was credit discrimination. Underestimating operating and/or marketing costs was a subsequent problem.[6]

Another study of 122 black, white, Hispanic, and American Indian women entrepreneurs found that the responses of both minority and nonminority women entrepreneurs differed significantly from those of women (nonentrepreneurs) in the general population on tests measuring achievement, autonomy, aggression, conformity, independence, benevolence, and leadership. Differences were also found between minority and nonminority women entrepreneurs, with minority entrepreneurs reporting that they started their businesses at a later age than the nonminority women.[7]

Twenty-one women who participated in a study of the demographic characteristics, motivations, and business problems of female entrepreneurs indicated that they had particular problems with collateral, obtaining credit, and overcoming society's belief that women are not as serious as men about business.[8]

Another study focused on how the characteristics of women entrepreneurs varied according to the type of business. Female entrepreneurs in nontraditional business areas (finance, insurance, manufacturing, and construction) also differed from their counterparts in more traditionally "female" business areas (retail and wholesale trade). The latter group had particular difficulty in gaining access to external financial sources, from banks, informal investors, or venture capitalists.[9]

A final study reporting the results of a nationwide in-depth survey of 468 women entrepreneurs profiled the "typical" woman entrepreneur.[10] She is the first-born child of middle-class parents—a self-employed father and a mother who does not work outside the home. After obtaining a liberal arts degree, she marries, has children, and works as a teacher, administrator, or secretary. Her first business venture in a service area begins after she is thirty-five, with her biggest problems being finance, credit, and lack of business training.

In some respects, women entrepreneurs possess very different motivations, business skill levels, and occupational backgrounds than do their male counterparts. The start-up process of a business for women entrepreneurs is also different from that of males, especially in terms of support systems, sources of funds, and problems. Men are often motivated by the drive to control their own destinies, to make things happen. This drive often stems from disagreements with the boss or from a feeling that they can run things better. In contrast, women tend to be motivated by a need for independence and achievement that results from the frustration they feel at not being allowed to perform on the job at the level they are capable of. Both men and women entrepreneurs feel their best solution to these problems is to venture out alone.

Start-up financing is another area in which male and female entrepreneurs differ. While males often list investors, and bank or personal loans in addition to personal funds as sources of start-up capital, women in nearly all cases have relied solely on personal assets or savings. This problem area will be discussed later: the difficulty most women have in obtaining lines of credit.

Occupationally, there are also vast differences between men and women entrepreneurs. Although both groups have had experience related to their ventures, men tend to be recognized specialists in their field or to be competent in a variety of business skills; the nature of their experience is often in manufacturing, finance, or technical areas. Most women, by contrast, usually have administrative experience, which is limited to the middle management level in the more service-related areas.

In terms of personality, there are strong similarities between male and female entrepreneurs: both tend to be energetic, goal-oriented, and independent. Men, however, are often more confident, and less flexible and tolerant than women, which can result in different management styles. This area is discussed in more detail in chapter 2.

The backgrounds of male and female entrepreneurs tend to be similar, except that most women are a little older when they embark on their venture (thirty-five to forty-five for women versus twenty-five to thirty-five for men) and their educational backgrounds are different. As has already been pointed out, studies indicate that male entrepreneurs frequently studied in technical or business related areas, while most women entrepreneurs were educated in liberal arts.

Support groups also provide a point of contrast between the two. Men usually have outside advisors (lawyers, accountants) as their most important supporters, with the spouse being secondary. Women consider their spouses to be their most important advisors, close friends next most important, and business associates third. More-over, women usually rely heavily on a variety of sources for support and information, such as trade associations and women's groups, while men are not as likely to seek as many outside supporters.

Special Problems of Women Entrepreneurs

All entrepreneurs have problems with their businesses during start-up and current operations. Obtaining credit, weak collateral position, and problems in financial planning tend to be the most pressing problems reported by women entrepreneurs (see table 1–3). While financing is a problem for every entrepreneur, the problem is often more acute for women entrepreneurs for two reasons.

First, women often lack a financial track record in business, which results in difficulties in dealing with lending institutions. When considering a request for funds, most commercial lending

Table 1–3
Major Problems in Start-up and Current Operations

Start-up Problems	Percentage of Women Polled	Current Operations Problems	Percentage of Women Polled
Lack of business training	30%	Lack of experience in financial planning	18%
Obtaining lines of credit	28%	Demands of company affecting personal relations	15%
Lack of experience in financial planning	20%	Weak collateral position	13%
Weak collateral position	21%	Obtaining lines of credit	11%
Lack of guidance and counseling	21%	Lack of business training	11%

institutions or venture capital firms are interested in the entrepreneur's track record. For a woman entrepreneur who lacks experience in executive management, has had limited financial responsibilities, and proposes a nonproprietary product, the task of persuading a loan officer to lend start-up capital is not an easy one. As a result, a woman must often have her husband cosign a note, seek a co-owner, or use personal assets or savings. Many women entrepreneurs feel strongly that they have been discriminated against in this financial area:

> Businesswomen are still treated as second-class citizens when it comes to the financial community.

A second reason that women often encounter difficulties in the area of finance is their lack of skills and experience in financial planning, accounting, marketing, and operations. Experience in dealing with money, negotiating and performing financial responsibilities, and developing expectations of being the boss inspires confidence in these areas. Most women entrepreneurs have backgrounds that did not give them the opportunity to develop confidence in business management and in negotiating financial matters. Generally speaking, most women entrepreneurs lack experience in finance, considering it their weakest business skill. This lack of experience and confidence in negotiating these matters in effect increases the risk in the eyes of the lender. Clearly, in order to gain access to outside capital, the woman entrepreneur must develop experience and confidence in dealing with finances and a well-organized business plan with clearly defined goals and objectives.

Unfortunately, sex stereotyping and continuing discrimination against women in the work force affect women business owners. Middle- and upper-level management positions in corporations are good training grounds for self-employment, but even though large corporations have hired more women in the past ten years, these women have not climbed the corporate ladder as far as have their male counterparts. The result is that even those women with corporate management experience have not had the same opportunity as many men to learn negotiating skills and to make important financial decisions.

Another area that women entrepreneurs often mention as a problem is the lack of respect for businesswomen. Entrepreneurs felt this particularly in the start-up phase of their business. One woman commented:

> There is a need for women to be taken seriously by the business and financial community.

This issue may be more apparent in fields where women business owners are fewer in number, but most important is the way women perceive themselves in their businesses and how each individual confronts the issue:

> I do not feel women are discriminated against if they are professional, knowledgeable, and above all, show a good degree of humility.

Another woman entrepreneur commented:

> Since I started the business in 1975, I have only been called 'honey' once. . . . I fired him.

Answers to Checklists

Answers to figure 1–1—Checklist for Feelings on Control:
If you answered yes to questions 4, 5, 8, 9, and 10, you seem to have the internal control necessary for entrepreneurship. Yes to questions 1, 2, 3, 6, and 7 indicates that external controls are holding you back.

Answers to figure 1–2—Checklist for Feelings on Independence:
Yes answers to items 1, 4, 5, 8, 9, and 10 indicate that you need to work on developing your own sense of independence more fully in order to compete in the business world.

Answers to figure 1–3—Checklist for Willingness to Take Risks:
Yes answers to questions 2, 5, and 9 indicate that you may need to work to develop a greater willingness to take risks.

2
Characteristics
of Women Entrepreneurs

My father never encouraged my sister or me just to work. He felt that you should have either a profession so that you could go on your own or something that would put you into your own business so that you would never have to be dependent on anyone else.

When growing up I saw how important it was to be independent—to be your own boss and to have control over yourself and your life. Values are more important than material goods. Chief values are truth, honesty, and the family. We are strongly attached to the church. We can express our values in our own business and still watch the business grow in terms of sales and profits.

These thoughts of two women entrepreneurs reflect aspects of their backgrounds. Many people today wonder: Who are the women entrepreneurs of the 1980s? What are their motivations and reasons for starting their own businesses? And what background experiences educationally and occupationally do they bring to their ventures? While the backgrounds of self-employed women vary considerably, these women share some similarities in personality, motivation, education, and family backgound.

Mary Phillips, a successful woman entrepreneur, is typical in many ways. She started working as a mail clerk for fifty dollars a week at the Bemis Bag Company in St. Louis, Missouri. Although she completed a few college courses in education, she decided not to become a schoolteacher like her mother and sisters and instead sought jobs in accounting and marketing. Following a divorce, she and her four children moved to Houston, Texas, where she was their sole support. There she settled on a career in commercial real estate. In 1972 the field was predominantly male and few firms employed women. Mary Phillips persisted and was eventually hired as the only woman among thirty-five men at a large, commercial real estate firm; her job was to make cold calls for the men. Mary's enthusiasm and tenacity paid off, and she did very well with the company. When she realized, however, that she was working as hard as her male counterparts and not being compensated at the same level, she resolved to establish her own real estate company.

> I started my business in 1978 on an initial investment of three thousand dollars after I was forced to give over a lead that I had to a male broker in the company. My client wanted to buy property near the Port of Houston. The male broker's commission on the sale was eighty thousand dollars. I was given a small referral fee of five thousand dollars.

Today Mary Phillips owns Phillips International, with offices in London, England, and Houston, Texas. Her income is over six figures and her company grosses more than $5 million annually. She believes that her assertiveness, hard work, and ability to be empathic have been important to her success. Her strong sense of independence and her marketing skills have also been assets.

Mary Phillips's case is typical in that her background influenced the nature of her business. We will next examine the composite characteristics of women entrepreneurs in terms of family, education, occupation, personality, motivation, and skills, both to understand women entrepreneurs generally and to help you to determine whether you should join the ranks and start your own business.

Background

Family

The family backgrounds of women entrepreneurs tend to be similar in many respects. The majority are first-born children from a middle- or upper-middle-class family in which the father was self-employed. Most of these women see themselves as similar to their fathers in personality, but as having a closer relationship with their mothers. Also over half of the women owning their own businesses are presently married to men employed in professional or technical occupations and have, on average, two teenage children.

What are the implications of this kind of background for the woman who wants to be an entrepreneur? For the women who fits the profile, there are basically three implications. First, being married and having a family frequently provides a support base, both emotionally and financially, from which to launch an endeavor. When the husband is professionally employed, the stress of relying on the new business for the family's financial support is also relieved. Balancing the dual roles of family and a business can create an extremely stressful situation and requires not only superior organizational skills on the part of the woman entrepreneur, but also a spouse who is encouraging and will help in managing a household. Cultural norms have encouraged men to divide their time among work, recreation, and family. For the woman business owner or the career woman, those time periods are seldom so distinct. Women often feel that even with a supportive and helpful spouse, it is their responsibility to organize for the household, family, and children. As a result, work and family are often fitted into available fragments of time, during which the woman's mind is never free from either concern. For the woman with the worries of her own business, with little time for recreation, this sense of fragmentation syndrome is often intensified.

Second, having a father who was self-employed provides a strong inspiration for the entrepreneur. The example set by the father of the independent nature and flexibility of self-employment is ingrained at an early age. Jeanie Ferrone of the Cellar Door, a discount designer shoe store, states:

> My father started and operated his own commercial airline. He was so consumed by the venture and provided such a strong example, it never occurred to me to go to work for anyone else.

Third, first-born children often become self-employed as they must learn at an early age to be assertive and independent. These characteristics are typical of both male and female entrepreneurs.

Clare Grosgebauer is a former teacher and freelance writer who owns a modest-sized advertising agency, Small Wonders, in the Washington, D.C., area. She was the only child in an upper-middle-class family, and her parents were both well educated. Her husband's profession as a lawyer has provided the stability for Clare to devote time to establishing her new venture in licensing children's products based on a story she wrote, "Snickerdoodle," and still care for her young daughter. She lists her father, a retired oil company executive, as very much like her in terms of personality and as her biggest supporter in the start-up of her business. Ms. Grosgebauer is typical of the large number of women entrepreneurs who are maintaining a delicate balance between work and family life.

> My biggest problem is the coordination of my family life and my business time-management. It is very difficult to find time to make overnight business trips. I have managed by setting priorities.

Priority setting is a key in balancing the dual roles of motherhood and business owner. It is discussed in chapter 3.

If your family background doesn't match this general profile, will it be an obstacle to your becoming an entrepreneur? Not really. For example, an unmarried woman without a family at home obviously does not face the conflicting demands of family and work. This situation can work to your advantage, as you will have more energy and will be able to devote your undivided attention to the business. Likewise, not having a self-employed father or being second- or fifth-born in a family will not affect the success or failure of the business. Moreover, there are always examples to be found in friends or relatives who can act as models of the experience of self-employment and provide inspiration for you.

One possible drawback to being single, however, is that your emotional and financial support bases may be weaker. Self-employment can be a very lonely experience, and close friends or colleagues are needed for support. In addition, the financial risk is higher, for you will have no second income to fall back on should the business be slow in turning a profit. But don't let this stop you if you are determined to be an entrepreneur, for the only real way to reduce the risks involved is to be as well informed and as well prepared as possible.

Education

> In my family, education was important. My mother was a dentist in a day when most women did not even graduate from high school.

For most women entrepreneurs, education was important in their upbringing, and it continues to play a major role in helping them to cope with deficiencies in their business skills. Nearly 70 percent of all women entrepreneurs have a college education, many with graduate degrees; their parents, particularly their fathers, and their spouses are also well educated. This situation is typical of middle-class families in which achievement and working hard to complete an education are emphasized. The most popular college majors among women are English, psychology, education, and sociology, with few taking degrees in engineering or science, but as more women come to recognize the stiff competition in the job market, they are choosing majors in business, science, and engineering.

Although a formal education is not necessary for starting your own business, any education specifically related to the field of the venture is obviously an asset. Still, for those women with a liberal arts background, the lack of an engineering or science background can be a problem in establishing a business in the traditionally male-dominated fields. As a result, most women entrepreneurs (90 percent) start service-related businesses. This will result in smaller firms occurring, for as we have already seen in chapter 1, the areas of new inventions and product/service modifications have the greatest growth potential.

Another obvious drawback for a woman having a liberal arts degree is a lack of business knowledge and skills. The major in psychology, sociology, or education teaches strong "people" skills, but a fundamental understanding of economics, finance, or marketing is often lacking. This can make launching a business more difficult for women and can cause a lack of confidence.

How can you correct these educational shortcomings? The majority of women entrepreneurs have compensated for their lack of business skills by taking business seminars or by seeking further formal education. This willingness to learn can turn a weakness into an asset, because taking a course, for instance, can provide solutions to immediate problems in the business and opportunities to update business techniques. The American educational system has traditionally discouraged women from concentrating in science, engineering, or computer technology, steering them instead toward areas like nursing or education; the realities of the marketplace may

cause schools and teachers to start treating girls and boys uniformly
and to avoid sex stereotyping of different fields in the future. This
may be little consolation if your education has left you unprepared
for the business world, but it is never too late for you to take a
course, learn basic accounting, and gain the skills you need to be an
entrepreneur.

Work Experience

The typical woman entrepreneur has had experience in the area of
her endeavor, usually in a service-related field, like teaching, middle
management, or secretarial. When women entrepreneurs continue
in the field in which they have experience (which is often the case),
they increase their chances of success. Not only can they avoid mistakes, but the psychic risk or fear of failure is decreased for the
woman who is confident in her knowledge of the business. Because
of the way they are socialized, women are often unaccustomed to
taking risks, so that by doing what they know best, they can eliminate many of the reasons for failure.

But unlike many male entrepreneurs, women entrepreneurs
often have limited previous experience. Even those with experience
in a business environment often lack skills in finance, general management, and manufacturing; this lack of skill, of course, lessens
their versatility and can create problems, especially when such
women decide to begin a business in an unfamiliar area.

Most women entrepreneurs have had experience in positions
where they could observe general managers or executives and see
them at their best and worst. This experience often provides a woman
the motivation to venture out alone in the first place, because she feels
she could "do a better job." This kind of job is a good training ground
and is a way to gain knowledge by, so to speak, "going to school on
someone else's mistakes." Nevertheless, being an observer is very different from being a doer. Women in these jobs lack the experience of
making management decisions, often because they have not been
given the opportunity, but this inexperience makes it difficult when in
starting their own businesses they are faced with such problems as
personnel difficulties, government tax regulations, and the necessity
of keeping clients happy. The following case illustrates how some
general management experience can be very helpful.

Nancy Donohoe spent three years as a part-time salesperson at various women's clothing shops selling better dresses, sporting clothes, and boutique items. In addition, she spent three more summer seasons managing one branch of a chain boutique. Her duties included hiring, financial planning, inventory, displays, and organizing a series of fashion shows. At thirty-nine years old, with her two children in junior and senior high school, Ms. Donohoe decided to go into partnership and plans to open her own store. Because she had "run someone else's business," she had a clear idea of what the keys to success for her new store would be. Before opening her store, Ms. Donohoe personally visited every clothing store in the northern New Jersey area she was considering, and she decided that a boutique-style children's shop offering unique children's clothing and gifts for the upper-income segment was the best opportunity for profit.

Besides doing her homework in advance, Ms. Donohoe is not afraid to be a manager. She has learned to discipline employees diplomatically, not to hesitate in marking down items that are slow to sell, and most important, to consider first the profits and costs.

Like Ms. Donohoe, if you plan to be an entrepreneur, you should obtain, if possible, general management experience before starting your own business. If this is not possible, you should make the most of your work experience by observing the general managers you work with, to see how they conduct their business, make decisions, and deal with problems.

Entrepreneurial Characteristics

Personality
In order to get a fuller picture of the personality and motivation of the woman entrepreneur, let us first consider how these entrepreneurial characteristics compare with those of the typical woman executive. The person making a career as a company executive usually has experience or expertise in her specific area, is conservative, cautious, logical, and averse to risk; these attributes are necessary for performing the more "custodial" tasks required within an organization, such as controlling cash, people, or assets. This kind of person is concerned with preserving and increasing the existing assets of the corporation and will not do anything unusual without careful

advance planning, which often includes consultation with others or a study of the options. The benefits of this kind of work include more regular hours, security, and a comfortable life-style.

In contrast, the woman entrepreneur is an individualist, creative, enthusiastic, instinctive, and adaptable. She must deal with very real and immediate problems like meeting payroll, hiring and firing employees, and pacifying creditors, often in the face of little cash, instability and few assets. An entrepreneur is not a cog in a wheel and cannot take the time to make lengthy studies or spend weeks seeking advice before making a decision. Her concern is for growth and creating assets. The rewards can be great both financially and psychologically, but the drawbacks can mean sacrifices personally, emotionally, and financially.

A high energy level is essential for the woman entrepreneur because the success and profits of the business depend on her efforts. Since she is the owner, the woman entrepreneur needs to inspire and motivate her employees. This calls for self-confidence and flexibility. And indeed, we hear these characteristics in the voices of the women entrepreneurs themselves:

> I consider myself to be very persistent and independent.

> I was determined to make my business succeed.

> I am outgoing, independent, and I make an effort to learn what I can about everything.

> I don't relate to failure. I am energetic, self-confident, and I work well under pressure.

As you can see from these comments, most women entrepreneurs possess the same general characteristics as the typical male entrepreneur. They are highly energetic, independent, self-confident, competitive and very goal-oriented. They are usually generalists rather than specialists and are more flexible than rigid. The characteristics of the woman entrepreneur refute the common opinion that women are strongly dependent and passive. In fact, the typical woman entrepreneur resembles her male counterpart in most personality areas. Figure 2–1 indicates a self-assessment of their personality characteristics by women entrepreneurs. The right-hand column lists those personality characteristics typically attributed to male entrepreneurs.

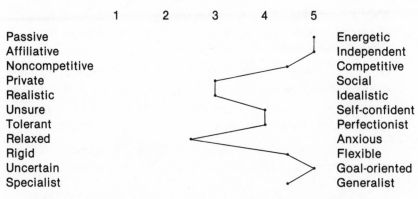

Figure 2–1. *Personality Characteristics of Women Entrepreneurs*

There are differences, however, between the profile of the traditional male entrepreneur and that of the woman entrepreneur. For one thing, women tend to be older (thirty-five to forty-five years old) when they start their first significant business venture, while the typical male entrepreneur is between thirty and thirty-five. This added life and family experience gives the woman entrepreneur a more realistic and pragmatic approach to their businesses, and the benefits of this experience are most valuable in the sales forecasts and financial projections of the company. Furthermore, this age factor, combined with the fact that most women entrepreneurs are married to men employed in professional or technical areas often paying more than fifty thousand dollars a year, greatly reduces financial anxiety. That the family's sole support does not depend on the success of the woman's venture allows the woman entrepreneur to have a more flexible management style and to place less pressure on co-workers and subordinates.

That women entrepreneurs see themselves as only moderately social on the private/social spectrum of figure 2–1 may reflect the view that overly social behavior can be detrimental to a woman's business image. Often an overly sociable woman is considered less serious about her business, whereas the sociable man is often considered just a good guy. Women entrepreneurs are not interested in receiving special treatment from their colleagues and in particular from male business associates. They only want to be treated with respect as competent business owners, without regard to personality traits that may be considered feminine or masculine. As one entrepreneur stated:

What I would like is acceptance in the business world as a businessperson without having to overcome the stereotypical views about women.

How have the personality traits typical of women entrepreneurs served them? Some women entrepreneurs consider their high energy level, assertiveness, and goal orientation vital to their success in establishing their businesses. In the words of one entrepreneur:

Don't waste time worrying whether qualities like independence, persistence, and goal orientation are not ladylike—use them to the fullest and prosper.

Recall the case of Ms. Phillips; her enthusiasm, hard work, and persistence were essential to her establishing a successful business in commercial real estate.

If you don't have all the personality traits of the typical woman entrepreneur, don't be discouraged. Not every present or budding entrepreneur meets the typical personality profile. Certain characteristics such as persistence, hard work, and goal orientation are prerequisites, but they usually evolve not from personality traits, but from a belief in an idea and a commitment to make that idea a reality. The real test is: are you willing to commit yourself and work very hard to make something you really believe in a success?

If you are contemplating starting your own business or are presently managing your own endeavor, you should reflect honestly on your personality strengths and weaknesses. This should help you to maximize your strengths and to put your talents to their best use. For example, if you feel unsure in your business decisions and consider yourself to be more social than private, you should use your people skills to cultivate guidance from a mentor or business associate and to develop confidence. Or if you are more a specialist than a generalist, a partnership arrangement or hiring a general manager would be in order for you.

Motivation
Although many people are motivated and have the background to start their own businesses, only a very few actually decide to take the plunge and start their own enterprises. A key barrier seems to be risk. If you are comfortable and secure in a situation, have a family

to support, a certain life-style and reasonably predictable free time, why risk all of this to venture out alone?

Risk can be broken down into three categories; financial, psychological (fear of failure), and social (fear of what others will say). Often the financial risk is most critical since most new businesses require more capital than expected before they can turn a profit. The psychological risk can be a big factor as well, especially for those who are unaccustomed to taking risks or who are starting their first business venture. Finally, social risk, especially as it relates to your family, can be important.

Women often have a more difficult time dealing with risk in its various guises. Many have not had the experience of being economically independent and are unaccustomed to taking financial risks. So, many women do not venture out alone until they are financially secure, either in terms of their own savings or the income of their spouses. Ann Hill of Design Works states:

> Women are socialized not to take chances or risks. Financially, they are eager to throw in the towel if it doesn't work because they are afraid to spend the extra money on an idea that may not work.

Another commented:

> A woman's whole socialization process makes her fearful of failure, fearful of success, and reluctant to take risks.

The psychological risk for women is often less because their motivation often has its roots in job frustration and interest in the area of the business. In addition, this risk is less since most women entrepreneurs start businesses in areas they know best:

> Why did I start my own business? Because of my professional experience, because I wanted to be independent, self-employed, and there was a need for my services.

Many women entrepreneurs feel this way. The most commonly cited reasons for starting one's own venture are interest in the area and job frustration. Other reasons, such as termination from a previous job, being widowed, and boredom are secondary in importance (see table 2–1). Curiously, job frustration combines with interest in the area (a positive and negative reason), to provide the

Table 2–1
*Motivations for Starting a Business
(ranked in order of importance)*

Independence
Job satisfaction
Achievement
Opportunity
Money
Status/prestige
Power
Economic necessity
Career security

usual catalyst. Why is this so common among women entrepreneurs? To begin with, many women are working in positions in which they have been loyal employees for several years. They reach a point where they feel they are at a dead end in terms of promotion, that they no longer have a vehicle for self-expression, or that they are no longer being challenged. This situation creates a strong sense of frustration and lack of job satisfaction.

A case in point is Vena Garrett. Ms. Garrett was a legal secretary for fifteen years before she and her partner started Rizzuti-Garrett, a consulting firm based in Irvine, California. Her new firm's specialty is providing in-house training and workshops on employee relations especially for secretaries and their bosses. The business is now six years old and was started with an investment of five thousand dollars; it was inspired by the owners' knowledge of these relationships, their own job frustration, and their seeing a need for such a service. States Ms. Garrett:

> We tried for many years (unsuccessfully) to offer our suggestions on secretary/boss team building in our own working environments. We finally decided we would have better luck on our own.

Given the experience and job frustration of most women, it is not surprising that the strongest motivators for starting their own businesses were the needs for independence, job satisfaction, and achievement. In other words, women entrepreneurs tend to be more interested in self-fulfillment than in money and power.

What is the effect of these circumstances on the business? First, that most women have had experience in the area of their own businesses means that they have spent time assessing the need for their product or service in addition to learning the business and gaining knowledge of the market. This experience helps the entrepreneur to be aware of such practical considerations as market opportunity, ability, and practice in providing the product or service. On the other hand, if the woman's motivation for starting a business was to get out of the house or to escape from problems in a marriage, the business is unlikely to solve the problem or to survive.

Second, the motivations of independence, job satisfaction, and achievement tend to be positive in the overall business context. For instance, a person who desires job satisfaction and achievement for herself will probably be more sensitive to those needs in her employees. Also, the drive for independence may make the business more creative, as the woman entrepreneur seeks to differentiate it from purely competitive businesses. Nevertheless, we must be careful not to overemphasize the quality of work life at the expense of the bottom line—profit.

Finally, motivations like the need for independence, job satisfaction, and achievement can create a strong determination to succeed. As Ms. Ferrone put it:

> I wasn't going to let myself fail. I was determined to succeed. I had the example of an entrepreneurial father, and I knew that with hard work I could do it. When I think back on all I did to create sales, going through parking lots and putting fliers on the windows of cars, for instance, I am amazed I ever succeeded.

Skills

Business management skills are something that every woman entrepreneur must assess before she starts her business. An assessment of strengths and weaknesses is essential because all too often the weaknesses will prevail if not recognized or compensated for in some way.

Most women entrepreneurs are very honest in assessing their skills. For the majority, finance is rated as very weak, marketing and business operations average, with strengths occuring in idea generation/product innovation and in dealing with people (see table 2–2).

Table 2–2
Women Entrepreneurs' Self-appraisal of Their Management Skills

Management Skill	Poor	Fair	Good	Very Good	Excellent	No Opinion
Finance—securing capital, forecasting, budgeting	15%	32%	27%	15%	6%	4%
Dealing with people—management, development, and training	2%	10%	28%	33%	27%	0%
Marketing/sales—marketing research, promotion, selling	6%	20%	20%	33%	22%	0%
Idea generation/product innovation	3%	10%	26%	27%	33%	1%
Business operations—inventory, production, day-to-day operations	3%	18%	32%	30%	17%	0%
Organizing and planning—business strategy, organizational structure, policies	4%	15%	29%	29%	23%	0%

This general assessment is caused by two factors: the lack of undergraduate business training among women, and the low level of experience in general management positions. As has been pointed out before, the majority of women entrepreneurs have a liberal arts education and work experience in positions where major marketing, financial, and business operating decisions were made by a superior. This results in a low skill level and a lack of confidence in key areas like finance and business planning. On the other hand, women entrepreneurs usually have solid experience and the accompanying confidence in the area of dealing with people.

How does this skill assessment affect the business of the woman entrepreneur? First, the low self-assessment of skills (and the actual lack of such skills) in finance, marketing, and organizing and planning may present a barrier to the future growth of the organization. As the business grows, it will be essential for the woman entrepreneur to plan strategically in order to accommodate expansion and increased sales, and to meet capital needs. For example, once a business is profitable and cannot increase sales without additional locations, geographic expansion in sales territory, or greater diversity in merchandise, the business owner must do two things: one, seek funding to accommodate expansion; and two, devote more time to the future of the business. Basically, she must answer the question, "Where do I want the business to be next year, and how am I going to get it there?" Accomplishing this task successfully requires a business track record and confidence in negotiating to obtain bank funds, as well as the ability to plan for the future by looking at the business environment and at the competition to determine how the business will survive in the future. Unless the problem of inadequate business skills is overcome through education, experience, or by hiring experts, the business may easily stagnate. Hiring experts is exactly what many women entrepreneurs do. Ms. Phillips of Phillips International says:

> I have always hired or rented intelligence in the areas where I was lacking.

Helen Richey of New Haven Bag and Burlap in Hamden, Connecticut, adds:

I recognized my weaknesses so I hired the best paid thinkers and attorneys possible.

Second, "average" skills in marketing and in business operations are not necessarily a drawback, depending on the nature of the business. Most of the businesses started by women are service-oriented and therefore require personal selling to some extent. Marketing skills such as those used in market research and forecasting probably do not need to be superior, because experts with these specialized talents can be hired. Similarly, business operations skills need to be strong rather than average in a business that is labor intensive, involved in manufacturing or construction, or providing complex and recurring personal services. For instance, while a production manager would require some operations and technical maintenance skills, such skills are not critical for a manager running a real estate office.

Third, the women entrepreneurs determined that strong management skill areas are dealing with people and idea generation/product innovation. These skills are definite assets. Strength in dealing with people can be especially helpful in working with employees and in negotiating with clients. Women tend to be more tolerant and understanding in the human relations side of running a business, which tends to make them more sensitive to problems and willing to work things out than men. Strength in idea generation/product innovation is helpful, for all entrepreneurs conceive an idea for their new product or service that has some unique features. If the first innovation does not work, a second or third innovation can be developed in order for the enterprise to thrive. Women entrepreneurs, like their male counterparts, love the enterprise and organization they created, not the innovation in itself.

3
Preparation for
Starting Your Business

Be better prepared—get some experience in the field, know your product, research your market, and be ready to work hard.

The best preparation is to run someone else's business first; then you understand the importance of organizing and prioritizing responsibilities.

Preparing to start a new enterprise involves many steps. As the above comments indicate, certain steps are more important for women entrepreneurs for two reasons: first, these steps will help in the successful establishment of the venture; second, the preparation will decrease the fear of failure that so many women entrepreneurs experience, giving them more confidence in the start-up phase of their business. Discussions with many women entrepreneurs suggest that the key preparatory steps include assessing motivation, assessing personal characteristics, organizing and prioritizing personal responsibilities, gaining occupational experience, establishing a track record, establishing a support system, and continuing education. The case of Betty Jo Toccoli illustrates the importance of this procedure.

Betty Jo Toccoli started Laura Lynn Cosmetics Manufacturing in Pacific Palisades, California, more than five years ago. Anyone entering a new business venture faces risks, frustrations, and problems, but for a woman trying to establish her own firm in this highly competitive industry, these concerns were intensified. What was key to Ms. Toccoli's success? First, her previous occupational experience.

Before starting Laura Lynn, Ms. Toccoli was vice-president of sales at a major personal care products company where she directed a sales force of more than one thousand people. In addition to experience in a wide variety of areas ranging from budgeting and personnel management to marketing and planning, she also had fifteen years of experience in the personal care products field. This background proved essential when she had to raise over eighty thousand dollars from ten private investors and set up procedures for more than four hundred independent sales representatives in sixteen states.

Ms. Toccoli was also very savvy in her selection of outside board members; she chose them on the basis of their areas of expertise. She believes that her personality, drive, and experience helped her to accomplish everything needed at start-up.

> I am easy to work with and always have a support plan, even though I don't make changes too quickly. My background in people skills was a definite asset.

Today her business is doing very well, with revenues over the $500,000 mark, and plans are being considered to expand into eastern markets.

Personal Assessment

Before you take any active steps toward setting up a business, take some time to evaluate your reasons for wanting to be an entrepreneur. You should also take into account your personality traits, realistically considering how they may help or hurt your business, to see whether in fact you are temperamentally suited to the life of an entrepreneur. Finally, you need to organize your personal responsibilities and establish priorities; if you are to be successful as an entrepreneur, you must be well organized.

What Is Your Motivation?
All women entrepreneurs should ask themselves this question: "Why do I really want to start my own business?" The possible answers range from an opportunity, need, and interest in the area,

to more negative reasons, like job frustration, divorce, or termination. Most women are motivated by a combination of reasons both positive and negative, but it is important for you to determine your true motivations.

> I was once in a seminar with another woman who was describing her motivation for opening a gift store. As she put it, she had no prior experience in the field, but thought the gift business might be a good idea now that she was single and felt she could borrow the money from her ex-husband.

This quote describes a woman entering a business endeavor for all the wrong reasons. She has no prior experience and has not organized her personal life. If she did obtain the money from her ex-husband, the fortunes of the business would hopelessly be tied to a personal and unsupportive relationship.

As a potential woman entrepreneur, you should make a list of all your motives for starting your own business, dividing them into positive and negative columns. When the list is complete, you should ask the following questions:

Are there entries on both sides?

Do the lists balance?

Are some reasons stronger than others?

Are there conflicts among the reasons?

Can you summarize your major motivation in one sentence?

The answers to these questions will help you to assess your real reasons for seeking self-employment.

Some reasons for not becoming an entrepreneur include:

I thought it would be fun.

I am single now and need a job.

I have more time—my children are grown.

None of these motives indicate the level of commitment necessary to make an idea for a new business successful. As we saw earlier, most women entrepreneurs list their main motivations for becoming self-employed as independence and achievement. These motivations are very positive as they relate to managing an enterprise; establishing a business, however, requires a strong desire to succeed and to make a profit. These motives and desires are not mutually exclusive because the business will not succeed if it is not profitable. So, the needs for achievement and independence through self-employment, and the knowledge that a better service is being provided are the intrinsic rewards that result from success, but they are not ends in themselves.

Janice Burling, of the Honeysuckle Hill Guest Inn in Massachusetts, put it this way:

> In assessing your motivation, make sure you're opening your own business for money; doing it only because you thought it would be fun can be an excuse for failure.

Also required are an interest in the area of the business and the existence of an opportunity in the market. You must enjoy the area you have chosen to be able to sell the product or service successfully, and of course there must be a niche or need for the product or service that you are offering.

Your Personal Characteristics

> *Women are not that much different from men in an entrepreneurial venture. They have a high energy level, dedication, training, the ability to motivate, and as good ideas as male entrepreneurs have.*

Several qualities are typical of most entrepreneurs. A woman entrepreneur, however, may find it difficult to assess her personal characteristics because she has fewer role models. How do you know if you "have what it takes?" Although the answer varies with the type of business, figure 3–1 gives a short exercise that may help you to understand the typical qualities of the woman entrepreneur and to see how you fit the profile. The answers are included at the end of the chapter.

Organizing and Prioritizing Personal Responsibilities

Once you have a clear idea of your motivation, you should assess your personal situation. The typical woman entrepreneur has a husband

and family, and even though most husbands tend to support their spouse's ventures, organization and prioritization of personal responsibilities can be helpful.

Some questions you should consider in assessing your personal responsibilities are the following:

Do I feel that my career and family should be kept separate?

How do I feel about delegating child care and household responsibilities?

Am I willing to spend extra time organizing and planning household duties?

Can I rely on friends and relatives to help out when I know I will be unable to reciprocate?

How does my husband feel about sharing household and child care responsibilities?

Will I be able to leave work at work and devote high quality time to my family?

Addressing these issues and discussing them with your husband and/or family will help you to remember that you cannot do everything—it is difficult to balance being a wife and mother and still run a successful business. If you feel that you are unable to balance these dual roles, you should reconsider very carefully the idea of starting a new enterprise. One woman entrepreneur commented:

Women need to realize that they don't have to be perfect, while men need to learn to accept women, their abilities, and achievement needs.

Unfortunately, women entrepreneurs often feel responsible for family and household duties even in two-career families in which both the husband and the wife work an equal number of hours per week. As a result, women tend to take less time for recreation and for themselves, instead dividing their hours between work and family. This situation can be very stressful and should be addressed in the preparation stage of the business. Here is a suggested list of

1. A woman entrepreneur is most commonly the _____ child in the family.

   a. oldest
   b. middle
   c. youngest
   d. doesn't matter

2. A woman entrepreneur is most commonly:

   a. married
   b. single
   c. widowed
   d. divorced

3. A woman entrepreneur usually begins her first significant entrepreneurial business enterprise at which age?

   a. teens
   b. twenties
   c. thirties
   d. forties
   e. fifties

4. A woman's entrepreneurial tendency first appears evident at which of these stages?

   a. teens
   b. twenties
   c. thirties
   d. forties
   e. fifties

5. Typically, a woman entrepreneur has attained the following educational level by the time she begins her first significant business venture:

   a. less than high school
   b. high school diploma
   c. bachelor's degree
   d. master's degree
   e. doctor's degree

6. A woman entrepreneur's primary motivation for starting a business is:

   a. to make money
   b. because she can't find a job working for someone else
   c. to be powerful
   d. to be famous
   e. to have an outlet for unused energy
   f. job frustration

7. The primary basis for the woman entrepreneur's self-confidence and need for achievement is her relationship with her:

   a. spouse
   b. mother
   c. father
   d. children

8. Women entrepreneurs typically form:

   a. service businesses
   b. manufacturing firms
   c. financial companies
   d. construction firms

9. Women entrepreneurs tend to be:

   a. generalists
   b. specialists
   c. planners
   d. inventors

10. A successful woman entrepreneur relies most on which of the following groups for important management advice:

   a. an internal management team
   b. external management professionals
   c. financial sources
   d. no one

11. Women entrepreneurs are:

   a. high risk takers (big gamblers)
   b. moderate risk takers (realistic gamblers)
   c. low risk takers (take few chances)
   d. doesn't matter

12. Women entrepreneurs:

   a. are the life of the party
   b. are bores at cocktail parties
   c. will never go to parties
   d. fit into the crowd at a party

13. Women entrepreneurs are:

   a. perfectionists
   b. opportunists
   c. good in human relations
   d competitive

14. For the woman entrepreneur:

   a. business is a top priority
   b. being in control is important
   c. need for achievement is a key motivation
   d. idealism is a common trait

Figure 3–1. *Characteristics of a Woman Entrepreneur*

household chores that women entrepreneurs should try to delegate or share among family members in order to cut down on stress and worry:

Paying the bills

Meal planning, grocery shopping, and cooking

Housekeeping

Clothes shopping for children

Child care—transportation and general care

Child care during illness

Laundry—washing and ironing

Household repairs and maintenance

Miscellaneous errands—dry cleaners, household items, gifts, and so forth.

Vacation planning

Investment planning

Once these practical considerations have been discussed, delegated, and settled, you should remember two basic things. First, train yourself not to worry about delegating responsibilities when hiring housekeepers or babysitters. Instead, screen these caretakers carefully, always interview and check references, and be sure that all responsibilities are mutually understood and clearly noted, preferably in writing. This process can often be difficult, as one woman entrepreneur found:

> I have gone through three stages—trying to do everything at work and at home; then delegating some things, but still worrying about them and continually checking up; and finally delegating and trusting with less worrying. This evolution is a function of experience as well as learning to trust my judgment and being absolutely clear about what I expect from people in the beginning.

The second thing women entrepreneurs should remember is to take time for themselves. It is easy to say, "I don't have time," but making some time for yourself is essential in maintaining an even keel. Women entrepreneurs should make special time for athletics, relaxing, hobbies, or reading, as do their male counterparts. Most male entrepreneurs make sure they take time periodically to attend a basketball game, read a novel, or play tennis.

As an entrepreneur, you must not be afraid to say no when called on to do extra things, like helping with the heart fund auction or baking cookies for the school. It is important to be selective about the choices you make and not feel guilty about them. The woman entrepreneur learns to overcome any guilt feelings, for she knows that she is doing the best she can in her dual roles. Moreover, spouses of women entrepreneurs can reduce guilt feelings by not expecting lavish thanks for every shirt they iron or meal they cook. Instead of feeling guilty, remember that you are contributing to the family's income and that families in which everyone is active and fulfilled are generally happier ones.

The key to maintaining this balance between the demands of family and work is organization. For both single and married women entrepreneurs, lists, phone message pads, time-saving pocket organizers, planning for the future, and contingency plans can be helpful. Also essential is the need to prioritize. When making a list of things to do, you should ask, "Which items are most important?" The highest-priority items should be accomplished first, for not everything can be done right away. Above all, when the organization comes apart, you need to have a sense of humor. Inevitably the children will get the chicken pox, or you'll be snowed-in in Buffalo, or the car will not start. When small disasters like these happen, the best solution is to look for the humor of the situation, and then begin to untangle the mess one stop at a time. One woman business owner offers this advice:

> It's been tough to balance my family with my new business, but I have learned to laugh at myself, otherwise I tend to take everything too seriously, and then I'm no fun to be with at work or at home.

Professional Preparation

If you have decided that the life of the entrepreneur is for you, you need to take steps to prepare yourself for starting a business. You may want to set up shop right away, but making preparations first will hep you to avoid some serious pitfalls.

Gaining Occupational Experience

> *Gain experience by managing another business before you start your own. It's the only way to discover if you have the ability and desire to be in charge.*

This is the advice that the majority of women entrepreneurs offer to anyone contemplating starting her own venture. As was the case for Betty Jo Toccoli, it is vital that you learn all aspects of running a business, from business skills in budgeting to personnel relations. If you have no previous managerial level experience, you will be at a distinct disadvantage. Everybody "learns on the job," but the woman at the managerial level who wants to be an entrepreneur must learn so much more.

Unfortunately, many occupations are still sex-segregated, and you may find it difficult to move beyond a certain level position into management. But be careful not to use this as an excuse. Margaret Hennig and Anne Jardim note in their book, *The Managerial Woman*, that all too often "women describe themselves as waiting to be chosen, discovered, invited, persuaded, asked to accept a promotion."[1] The obvious question to ask, then, is: "Why not stop waiting and start acting?" As a potential woman entrepreneur, you should make sure that people understand your goals and that you are prepared to work hard to accomplish them. If you find yourself in a position where you are not getting the experience you want, you must assert yourself to gain that responsibility.

Some things you should try to learn while in a management position to gain experience include:

1. *Budgeting.* Develop a sense of how costs and sales operate within a budget. Understand variances and how qualitative items can have indirect costs.

2. *Personnel.* Attempt to gain experience in all aspects of personnel management, from screening and interviewing employees to delegating and directing to terminating.

3. *Negotiating.* Experience in negotiating for an idea, for money or for a specific proposal is always helpful because you learn the value of compromise and to separate personal concerns from business decisions. Learning these things is an asset, because in your own business you will seldom obtain all the inventory you want, all the money you need, or all the labor you require.

4. *Marketing.* Understand the functions involved in marketing; there is more to it than just selling. Participation in market research, public relations, or any personal selling effort is essential. Learn how the product, price, distribution, and promotion aspects of the business are intertwined, and gain

experience with customers to understand how their needs are satisfied.

5. *Decision Making.* Seek autonomy in making decisions. The ability to decide on an issue, carry it through to positive or negative results is very important. As an employee, you can seek advice from others. As a business owner, you are on your own and the fortunes of the business may be at stake. Learn how to collect relevant information, make the choice, act on it, and not look back.

If managerial experience is not possible, you can do several things to increase the breadth of your managerial skills as a lower-level employee.

1. Indicate to your supervisor that you are interested in learning more about a specific area, such as finance, marketing, or hiring. Ask if you can assist in preparing a report or collecting information on the subject. This will give you exposure to other important areas.

2. Be observant. Literally to go to school in your business by watching what the managers do and how they do it. For instance, how do they go about hiring, training, and managing new employees? What is their decision-making process? Do they operate within their budget? How do they respond to crises? You can learn a great deal through observation.

3. Attempt to gain experience running something. There are always opportunities both work-related and outside of work where you can be president or in charge of an operation. For example, at work you may find a special project that you can chair; outside of work you can find a consumer issue, a union project, a research study, or even organization of an extra-curricular activity. Any one of these will require decision making and organizing. Outside of work there are also businesswomen's professional groups, volunteer organizations, trade associations, and church groups. All these groups have committees requiring officers, and as an officer you can gain experience.

Finally, in addition to managerial experience, you should gain experience in the field you plan to enter, for you must be knowledgeable about the industry and about market opportunities. Ms. Donohoe, who will soon be opening a children's boutique in New Jersey, comments:

> My partner had no retail experience in her background at all when we agreed to start our children's boutique. She had years of experience in running her own dance company, but did not know much about retailing. She determined that the best way to learn was to get a job in a children's shop, learning from the bottom up. Now I think she knows the merchandise and customer group as well as I do.

As this case illustrates, your level of experience is less important than working in the industry to learn how it operates.

Establishing a Track Record

The single most important step in preparing to start a new venture is to establish a track record and gain experience in dealing with money. Whether you are a twenty-year-old college graduate or a fifty-year-old manager making a career change, this step is essential in arranging start-up funding. Most women have not been brought up expecting to be their own source of financial support and often have more difficulty than men in learning how to negotiate financial matters. One woman entrepreneur says:

> Women lack early life experiences with money as a resource and expectations of being the boss.

But money matters need not pose a major obstacle for you, because it is never too late to learn about them.

How do you gain experience dealing with money and establish a track record if you have never owned a business? Here are some suggestions from some women entrepreneurs:

1. *Manage your family finances.* Set up budget, establish your total income and total expected expenses for the year. Check on the variations monthly and adjust the budget up or down

as necessary. This will give you some basic experience with budgeting and planning.

2. *Do your own family taxes.* Tax laws are complex, and by familiarizing yourself with your own taxes, you can overcome your initial fears and prepare for dealing with taxes in your business. You should understand that no one except tax experts fully understands the laws, but familiarity with terms, penalties, and forms is good preparation.

3. *Establish credit in your own name.* You should obtain credit cards, charge accounts, checking accounts, and insurance policies in your own name. These will help you to build a credit record. A good way to do this is to take out a personal loan to buy a car, property, or equipment, and pay it off. You will also gain exposure to bank lending processes and a good credit rating.

4. *Obtain experience bookkeeping through volunteer work or trade associations.* Valuable experience can be gained by functioning as a treasurer or bookkeeper for your church, a volunteer organization, or any other association. You can gain a basic understanding of debits and credits, and add to your resumé.

One entrepreneur describes her experience in building a track record:

> I took out a two-thousand-dollar loan to do some household renovations even though I didn't need the money. My purpose was to learn how the loan process worked and to establish credit since I was new in town. When I returned to take out a business loan, I was better prepared.

In another case, Dr. Lynne Mofenson-Katz, a pediatrician, was required by the telephone company to put down a substantial deposit before being granted a business line because she had no previous track record.

Most important, make sure that you have no bad debts in your credit history as they can be more harmful to you than no history at all. Such bad debts in a credit history can include outstanding loans, or charge accounts that were not paid in the specified time period or were turned over to collection agencies. The local credit bureau can give you further information on your credit rating. If you have unpaid debts in your credit history, you should pay them off to clear your record.

Creating a Support System

> *From the beginning, my husband, family, friends, and clients were supportive, helpful, and fair with me. This increased my determination to succeed.*

Moral support is important at all stages in starting and running a new venture, but during the preparation stage, it is vital. Indeed, the lack of support may be a reason for deciding not to follow through. A woman entrepreneur's determination and confidence are often correlated with the support she receives from those close to her. Starting a venture is very lonely, and unless you have encouragement, it is easy to say "maybe this is not a good idea."

Moral Support—Family and Friends. Many women entrepreneurs would adapt the phrase "behind every successful man is a strong woman" to "behind every successful woman entrepreneur is a supportive man." The majority of women entrepreneurs indicate that their spouses, boyfriends, or fiancés are their biggest supporters. Gaining this support is important, because if this individual is not encouraging, he may have trouble accepting the new constraints on your time. If you find yourself in this situation, you should determine whether: he simply thinks that the idea for your business is poor; he resents the demands on your time; he feels threatened by your success; or he thinks that you lack the ability to make the business work. You should identify the basis for his objections and try to secure support in order to relieve undue pressures on yourself.

Friends are a key element in this moral support system. Many women entrepreneurs indicate their hesitancy to discuss a new idea with friends for reasons such as fear of criticism or a lack of understanding, but friends can offer encouragement and provide household or child care assistance. Friends can also provide advice and opinions that are often more honest than those from other sources.

But be sure you remember the context of the friends' opinions, because as friends they may be biased in your favor.

Relatives, including children, grandparents, parents, aunts, uncles, and cousins can also be a strong source of moral support. A relative who is also an entrepreneur will even be more understanding and supportive. As one entrepreneur stated:

> Total family support was the reason for my success. Having continued encouragement and understanding gave me the confidence to overcome all hurdles.

Professional Support—Finding a Mentor. The preparation stage of a business start-up is the best time to find a mentor. A mentor-protégée relationship can offer an added dimension; it can be a source of moral support as well as business guidance. Over 30 percent of women entrepreneurs have mentors.

Who are mentors and how do you find one? This is often not as difficult as it seems. The kinds of people who are self-employed in fundamental business activities like law, finance, or management are therefore well qualified to guide you in the "how-tos" of business establishment. In most cases, women seek mentors to balance the business skills in which they are deficient.

To start looking for a mentor, make a list of any experts you know from work or socially with whom you are fairly friendly. Does anyone on the list possess skills that would help you overcome a hurdle in your start-up? Do any people on the list possess expertise in an area in which you are weak? Do any of those on the list have long experience in the industry you plan to enter? If so, pick the person who can offer the most assistance and ask if you can discuss the new venture with her. If she is interested, she will tell you. You should present yourself as someone worthy of listening to, and it is up to you to follow through by keeping that person informed as to your progress in order to develop the relationship. A mentor should be viewed as a coach, an advocate, or a key supporter—someone with whom you can share both problems and successes in the venture. One woman entrepreneur outlines the function performed by her mentor:

> I met my mentor while working at an internship in retail management. He took a special interest in my desire to open my own store

and provided business training, coaching, tutoring, education in the retail industry, and taught me skills in all aspects of business. He was my confidant as well as my friend.

You may want to consider the mentor as a possible investor. As an investor, your mentor would have added incentive to participate in and offer guidance to the new venture.

A role model can serve a function similar to that of a mentor. Although not as many female as male role models are to be found, you can establish objectives and learn by observing someone who has "made it." Role models should be thought of in terms of how they got to where they are, how they manage their businesses, and what preparations they made beforehand to establish their businesses. A good role model has done many things right.

Furthering Your Education
Continuing education is important for a woman entrepreneur beginning a new business. It builds knowledge and thereby develops confidence in your ability to make the business succeed. You may want to learn new business skills or train in technical or practical studies in the area of your venture, but either kind of learning can give you a foundation on which to build. Just understanding the terminology in finance or advertising or having an extra class in retailing, counseling, or computer science can give you an edge in business start-up.

Although most women entrepreneurs have a broad liberal arts background, since the passing of Title IX of the Education Amendments of 1972, women have had equal access to the study of business, agriculture, medicine, and engineering. As a result, the number of women studying in more technical fields has increased by 5 percent to 15 percent; nevertheless, studies show that most women are taking degrees in nontechnical areas:

> Although women made gains in agriculture, architecture, business and management, and engineering, the greatest number of women are still receiving degrees in fields that have traditionally attracted the largest number of women, such as education and social sciences.[2]

One explanation may be that many women have been encouraged by guidance counselors to enter these traditional fields, where a liberal arts background can be an asset.

However, a liberal arts background can make it difficult for you to obtain economic independence; a more technical education may better prepare you for a business career. For example, Katie Whipple, a woman entrepreneur who founded a computer software company had a degree in math and a master's degree in aeronautical engineering, plus technical experience writing programs. This background, combined with her "workaholic tendencies," led to the successful establishment of a software company that has sales of over $10 million per year.

How can a potential or present woman entrepreneur "beef up" her education? Here are some sources where you can check on the availability of seminars, courses, or conferences:

Local college—continuing education, evening college, and day school

Adult education courses

Chamber of Commerce

SCORE—Service Corps of Retired Executives

Small Business Development Centers

Small Business Association

Banks and brokerage houses

Professional women's groups such as the Business and Professional Women's Organization or the National Association of Women Business Owners

Trade associations

There are more than 250 colleges and universities across the country offering courses in entrepreneurship or small business management; this figure represents an increase of 56 percent since 1980. Most of these courses take a pragmatic approach, rather than emphasizing theory or academics, and offer students the chance to develop an idea for a business, prepare a business plan, and in some cases run a student business on campus. In addition, many schools offer entrepreneurship clubs, which are valuable forums for comparing notes, airing ideas, and discussing problems. Entrepreneurship courses are even being taught in some high schools. Most are designed to give students a chance to participate in all aspects of running a business, from accounting and manufacturing to marketing and personnel management. Finally, self-education through reading books is always an excellent way to learn new skills. Appendix II provides a listing of books that may be helpful.

Any of the sources listed here may offer a seminar or class that would be relevant and affordable. One woman entrepreneur offers the following advice:

> Continue to learn; take minicourses or seminars whenever you can, as they will help you to make weaknesses in your business skills strengths, force you to plan and think of issues external to your venture, and more important, stimulate your enthusiasm.

Your Professionalism and Determination

It is very important for women entrepreneurs to be taken seriously in their business ventures. As we saw in chapter 2, women entrepreneurs tend to be similar in many respects to male entrepreneurs, with differences in only a few areas. High energy level, independence, and goal orientation are the qualities most women entrepreneurs consider essential.

Most women entrepreneurs (like most people) cannot change their personality traits past a certain point, which brings us to some related issues—determination and professionalism. Ms. Richey of New Haven Bag and Burlap states:

> Appearances are very important in business. A straightforward, down-to-earth approach and the confidence to say what you know are essential to being taken seriously about your business.

Being determined to bring your idea to fruition and doing so in a professional manner gives a woman entrepreneur credibility. How can you accomplish this?

First, while determination cannot be taught, it is often derived from a commitment to make something a reality. A women entrepreneur must believe in what she is doing and learn to deal with frustrations by motivating herself to overcome the inevitable obstacles.

Self-employment is a lonely experience involving many sacrifices, and without determination quitting is easy. There is always a way to overcome difficulties, and many entrepreneurs consider persistence the key to their success. When faced with an obstacle, you should ask, "Is this a good reason to give up?"

Professionalism is a second area that women entrepreneurs must consider. All women business owners should conduct themselves in a manner that will give credibility to their businesses. Women in atypical fields like construction or finance will be scrutinized more closely than will their male counterparts, increasing the necessity for professional behavior. Exactly what is "professional behavior"? The term is difficult to define, since there are certain informal rules that vary from one industry to the next. For instance, in banking, a gray suit is considered part of a "professional" appearance, whereas in the film industry Levi's may be *de rigueur*. At the risk of stating the obvious, here are a few rules that translate in all industries as professionalism:

> Be prepared with reports, statistics, or recommendations whenever you attend a meeting.
>
> Be punctual at all times.
>
> Be neat and well groomed at all times.
>
> Keep your family problems at home.
>
> Follow through—if you say you will do something, or will call back, or will send the check, then do it promptly.
>
> Accept criticism constructively rather than emotionally.
>
> Be yourself—do not try to be someone you are not.

By following these rules, you can establish credibility with employees, clients, and colleagues in the industry. Some women business owners made the following comments:

> Being professional is knowing your product or service backwards and forwards.
>
> Speak up and acknowledge that you are a woman running a business and doing a good job. Don't have any fear of saying you don't know something but will try.

Women must base decisions on realities rather than on emotional responses. Try not to take criticism personally and be more tolerant of situations.

Another part of professionalism is not letting gender be an issue in failures or mistakes. You should remember that you are a professional business person and expect to be treated as such. As one woman entrepreneur advises:

Women should not look at themselves as "women" anything. You're an entrepreneur or an employee, period. Your gender is irrelevant in your career but all-important privately. Do not let your gender be a crutch or excuse for failure.

Overall, preparation is a major step in establishing a new business. Research and experience in the proposed field is essential, and evaluating yourself in relation to the issues discussed in this chapter, from motivations to moral support systems, will help you to avoid future problems. At the preparation stage, there are many unknowns and often knowledge and enthusiasm for the venture are all you have to start with. Taking the endeavor to start-up is where the financial risk becomes a factor, where you have something real to lose, and at this point you will understand why decreasing your psychological risk through solid preparation is a good idea.

Answers to Characteristic Assessment

1. a	8. a
2. b	9. a
3. c	10. b
4. a	11. b
5. c	12. d
6. f	13. c
7. c	14. c

Scoring

10–14 correct	You have a very good understanding of key characteristics and a realistic view of the woman entrepreneur.
7–9 correct	You have a fair understanding of the typical characteristics.
6 or fewer	You have an unrealistic view of the characteristics typical of the woman entrepreneur and should do further personal assessment before starting a business.

4

Starting Your Business

Decide whether it is worth the sacrifice to start your own business. Evaluate the trade-offs: the time, the commitment, the insecurity of doing it on your own. It is a very individual choice and one to be made with much thought.

I had problems obtaining credit and establishing credibility. You have to be better than a man and must have more data to support your point.

These two women entrepreneurs mention some of the issues that should be raised before you actually launch a new enterprise. The need for careful planning and preparation was acknowledged by Lynn Walsh when she started A Sailor's Valentine. Lynn spent ten years working in the cosmetic division of Filene's Department Stores. She worked not only as a liaison between management and all Revlon concessions throughout the fifteen-store system in Massachusetts, Rhode Island, and New Hampshire, but also as a trainer, a buyer, and a department manager for the Revlon concession. Even though her original experience and her business (an art gallery on Nantucket Island, Massachusetts) were in unrelated fields, Lynn had learned how to determine the need for her product line, conduct a demographic study, and estimate inventory needs and cash flows. In her start-up phase, she went to the library, town halls, urban development and economic development offices and obtained statistics on income, competitive businesses, and on the art industry in particular. Next, she estimated her profits and losses and went to the bank to see how much they would loan her. She then projected a five-year cash flow, went back to the bank, and negotiated a ninety-day note for fifteen thousand dollars, on which she managed to pay 60 percent down at the due date. She was able to renegotiate an additional 120 days and rewrite the balance at current rates. Because of her planning and preparation, she has never had major difficulties in securing credit. In her third year of operation, she managed a revolving credit arrangement with the bank, even though the nature of her business is highly seasonal.

As Ms. Walsh's experience demonstrates, many important elements are involved in starting the new venture. Besides establishing a good business support system, you should evaluate various sources of capital and develop a solid business plan that includes a marketing plan, a financial plan, and an organizational plan. Moreover, each of these plans must be developed with an awareness of the legal issues involved in organizing the enterprise, and an understanding that starting a new business is generally more difficult for women than men. One government report stated:

> It has conclusively been shown that women business owners encounter more obstacles and face more risks, financially, socially, economically, culturally, and legally than men business owners face.[1]

This increased level of difficulty was elaborated on in another report:

> A systematic history of overt discrimination starts her on a course that steers her from a traditional "man's province," prevents her from training for careers that lead to entrepreneurship, diminishes her ambitions and aspirations for this career, and then places obstacles in her path as she tries to pursue it.[2]

Establishing a Support System of Business Associates

The adversities faced by the woman entrepreneur can be at least partially offset by establishing a strong moral support system of family and friends, clients and business associates. We described the importance of moral support in the previous chapter. Equally important to the new entrepreneur, however, is the need to develop a group of clients, business associates, and experts who can act as both a cheering squad and sounding board. Associates often provide the moral support for the woman entrepreneur to persevere when she is having difficulty gaining acceptance as a business person.

Some women entrepreneurs believe that their support systems were vital in helping them overcome their problems at start-up. Claudia Tischler of Quadra Construction is atypical of the majority of women entrepreneurs in that her business is in a male-dominated industry. Friends, relatives, and business partners make up her support system. Ms. Tischler believes that her success in establishing the business is directly related to her hard work, support systems, and decisions to take risks:

> In addition to knocking on a lot of doors and doing a better than average job, I found that building a support group, being a risk taker, and spending the money to do it right made the difference in my venture. The support I gained from trade and women's professional groups gave me the incentive to be disciplined to work hard every day.

What kind of business associates should you seek out for support? One group is made up of people who are themselves self-employed; they too have had the experience of starting a business. Besides this group, there are four major categories of people you should consider. First, there are clients or buyers of your product or service; second, suppliers—the companies or individuals who supply your business with goods, materials, and so on; third, there are experts—lawyers, accountants, and consultants; and finally, colleagues or associates from trade associations, networking or professional groups. Individuals from these groups can offer different kinds of support and guidance.

Client Group

The client group is an important group to cultivate. In addition to being your source of revenues, this group can help to establish "good will" toward your business. It also provides word-of-mouth advertising by satisfied customers and the direct feedback on all aspects of your product or service. By seeking the opinions of clients on a proposed product or service, you can create interest and support for your business. Customers, happy to see your concern for meeting their needs, can give you valuable feedback and they will probably be more loyal to the product/service. Eventually, all of this interaction will translate into greater profits for your venture.

Supplier Group

The supplier group is another important component of the business support system, for suppliers help to establish your credibility with creditors and customers. All businesses need a solid track record with suppliers. A woman who establishes business accounts that are paid promptly or that will extend credit will provide a bank with more information to consider when it evaluates a loan application for her business. In addition, you should build a relationship with suppliers in order to maintain adequate inventory and materials. Without this good source of supply, customers and creditors alike may question the viability of the business. Suppliers can also offer important advice on how the industry works, what the competition is up to, and what the general trends are. If possible, try to develop reciprocal arrangements with suppliers, as such arrangements can benefit both businesses.

Experts

The third group in the business support system is made up of experts, such as lawyers, accountants, consultants, or insurance advisors. These people are usually peripheral to the business venture itself, but they often have objective opinions on the workings of a business as it relates to their field, and thus can be very helpful as sounding boards for issues that may involve financial risks. So, it is particularly important for you to seek experts as supporters, especially when such unsettled matters as patent protection or tax laws are at issue.

Trade Associations, Professional Groups, Networking

Finally, business associates or acquaintances that you have met through trade associations, professional groups, or networking can be another important source of support. This group can provide an extension of the moral and emotional support you receive from family and friends, but with one major difference—business acquaintances are in business too and often have more empathy and understanding for the problems another business owner may encounter. A recent *Wall Street Journal* article illustrates the point nicely.

> At a recent Monday session, which began about 6 p.m. and lasted 3½ hours, a woman was angry about a dispute with a subcontractor.

He had filed a $1 million lawsuit to harass her, but was willing to settle for considerably less. Her lawyer advised settling because it would be cheaper than going to court. But she didn't want to pay anything, she said, because the subcontractor had violated their agreement.

The [networking] group told her not to let her anger stop her from doing what was best for her business. She should pay the settlement and get the problem behind her, they advised.[3]

In this case, the woman entrepreneur received good business advice (the good of the business takes priority) and moral support (the group agreed on the suggested course of action) at the same time. Even though the subcontractor may have been found guilty of violating the agreement, the time and costs spent in the court obtaining this decision were not worth the negative impact on the business. In a case like this one, support from business associates can reduce the anxiety of feeling completely alone. In a support group, you will meet other people who have problems and concerns similar to your own.

Setting Up a Business Plan

The importance of having a business plan can hardly be overstated. The business plan not only serves as a mechanism for obtaining any needed financial resources, but also indicates the future direction of the company. By helping you to determine this future direction, the plan can provide guidance in making daily decisions. In preparing a business plan, you should take into account the advice of one woman entrepreneur:

Don't get bogged down in details. Research the basics, but don't let the lack of information be an excuse for not starting your own business.

While this is a bit of an overstatement, do not be discouraged by the lack of information in the business plan, particularly the marketing data. The prime purpose of the business plan is to define and describe the business, indicating the direction the enterprise will take in the future. It is composed of three major parts: the marketing plan, the financial plan, and the organizational plan.

Some readers may be surprised to learn that a very difficult aspect of the business plan for the woman entrepreneur to decide on is "What business am I in?" The answer to this question guides the direction of the business by defining the products and markets of the company, the customers to be served, and the method for satisfying their needs. These definitions can become the guiding principles behind the organization, from the largest conglomerate to the smallest storefront operation. For example, International Business Machines is guided by these principles: respecting the individual; performing every task in a superior manner; and maintaining the best customer service in the world. Digital Equipment Corporation has these objectives: produce the highest quality products, and serve the customer. And American Telephone and Telegraph has these: service, service, service.

One woman entrepreneur indicated the importance of having a good business definition:

> As long as we understand that our business mission is to make the highest quality running shoes for runners, we are all right. It is when we forget this principle and attempt to compete with Nike that we get into trouble.

Despite its importance, the weakest area of the business plan for most women entrepreneurs is probably a concise definition of the product and market scope of the enterprise.[4] This weakness is evaluated as a very negative factor by potential sources of capital, and may well be one of the major reasons for a rejection of the woman entrepreneur's loan application. In the words of one bank manager:

> How can I loan money to a business when I am not certain she knows the business she is in and where it is going?

Once you have defined the business, you should describe it further. Answering the following questions can help you formulate a good description:

> Is your business primarily manufacturing, merchandising, or service?
>
> What are your primary products/services?
>
> Who are your target customers?

What geographic area do you intend to serve?

What will be special about your business?

Why will you be successful in this business?

What is your experience in this field of business?

What will be the form of the business—sole proprietorship, partnership, or corporation?

Why is your business going to be profitable?

How do you intend to serve your customers?

By answering these questions, you can develop an overall description of the business to be used in the business plan, the specifics of which will be detailed in the following sections.

A suggested outline for a business plan is given in table 4–1. This outline incorporates the major areas that you should consider in all aspects of the business plan, and suggests the organization of the data.

The Marketing Plan

By far the most difficult to develop and yet most important part of the business plan is the marketing plan. Surprisingly, little if anything has been written on this subject. As one woman entrepreneur said:

> I used several library books and articles, but found they were deficient in outlining exactly what marketing plans were, when to do one, why to do one, and how to use it.

You should view the marketing plan as the blueprint for the future direction of your enterprise. It is an important document to use in obtaining funds; it also provides a framework for decision making. Understanding what a marketing plan can and cannot do will help you to see its importance (see table 4–2). Although the market plan can do many things, it is not a crystal ball that will guide every decision and prevent mistakes. Nor should it be viewed as something carved in granit and therefore impossible to modify.

In developing this plan, you should understand some of the major difficulties involved.[5] The problems will of course vary from one

Table 4–1
Business Plan Outline

Cover sheet
  Name of business
  Names of principals
  Address and telephone number of business

Statement of purpose (executive summary)
  Description of business—product or service
  Business structure
  Description of:
    amount of money being requested
    how funds will be used
    how funds will be repaid

Marketing plan
  The industry
  The competition
  Market size and opportunity
  Market segments served
  Marketing mix
  Key factors to success in market

Financial plan
  Sources and applications of funds
  Capital equipment list
  Balance sheet
  Break-even analysis
  Income statements
  Pro-forma cash flow statements

Organizational plan
  Location of business
  Organizational structure
  Management
  Non-management personnel

Summary
  Application and expected effect of loan on business

Supporting documents (as required)
  Personnel resumés
  Job descriptions
  Credit reports
  Letters of reference
  Copies of contracts
  Copies of leases
  Copies of letters of intent
  Legal documents
  Production requirements

Table 4–2

What Market Planning Can and Cannot Do

Can Do	Cannot Do
It will enhance the firm's ability to integrate all marketing activities to maximize efforts toward achieving the corporate goals and objectives.	It will not provide a crystal ball that will enable management to predict the future with extreme precision.
It will minimize the effects of surprise from sudden changes in the environment.	It will not prevent management from making mistakes.
It establishes a benchmark for all levels of the organization.	It will not provide guidelines for every major decision. Judgment by management at the appropriate times still will be critical.
It can enhance management's ability to manage, since guidelines and expectations are clearly designated and agreed upon by many members of the marketing organization.	It will not go through the year without some modification as the environment changes.

Source: Robert D. Hisrich and Michael P. Peters, *Marketing Decisions for New and Mature Products* (Columbus, Ohio: Charles E. Merrill Publishing, 1984), 79.

woman entrepreneur to the next, but most will experience difficulties to some extent in obtaining needed information, doing the forecasting, and finding the needed time to put the plan together.

To begin with, you should obtain information regarding industry attractiveness, consumer needs and market composition, product availability, and data on competitive products and strengths. Remember, though, that it's rarely possible to obtain all the information you would like. Instead of letting this discourage you, look at it as a challenge to gain as much market information as possible.

Once you have accumulated the available information through government statistics, trade journals, or original research, you should try to make realistic forecasts for your particular market and product. Making such forecasts is difficult even for established companies in today's turbulent, competitive environment, so it is no wonder that this can be a problem for an entrepreneur just starting out. Nevertheless, these forecasts are crucial for two reasons: (1) they are scrutinized by potential investors, and (2) they establish the goals for your final marketing plan.

Gaining information and making forecasts are difficult enough, but the problems of performing these tasks are compounded by the time constraints you may well face. With so many demands on your time as you start a new enterprise, you may not have enough time to prepare the market plan as thoroughly as you might like. Nevertheless, you must set aside some time for this job if the new enterprise is to flourish.

In light of these difficulties, you may find it helpful to have an overview of the entire planning process before you consider each of the individual components of the plan. An overall framework for developing the market plan (shown in figure 4–1) indicates that the plan must start with a critical evaluation of the market/product situation and the possible strengths and weaknesses of the company. This analysis will then form the basis for establishing objectives, a process to be followed by the development and implementation of the marketing programs to reach these objectives. The starting point for the critical evaluation of the market/product situation is a general industry analysis.

General Industry Analysis. In analyzing an overall industry to find an opportunity for a business venture, you should evaluate several dimensions of the industry as a whole, as well as specific companies within the industry. Using the industry evaluation form shown in figure 4–2, evaluate each industry to the extent possible in terms of the environment, the buyers and their behavior, the products, production, pricing, distribution, and promotion. Each of these dimensions, of course, has several components. Not every category will be important to each woman entrepreneur's business, so select the categories important for your business from the table and obtain as much information as possible using the marketing research approach that will be developed later in this chapter. You know your new venture better than anyone else and are better able to determine the factors most critical for success. You should examine the overall competitive environment in the initial industry analysis, but this area is important enough to warrant a more in-depth evaluation in preparing the market plan.[6] This analysis can be done on an overall company basis and on a product/market basis using the worksheets in figures 4–3 and 4–4 respectively. On a company

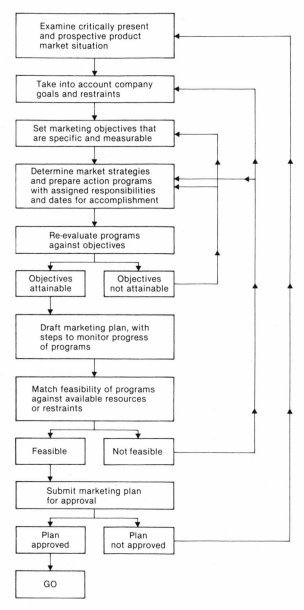

Source: David S. Hopkins, *The Marketing Plan* (New York: The Conference Board Inc., 1981), 17.

Figure 4–1. *Flow Chart for Developing a Market Plan*

Industry

Category	Company A			Company B			Company C			Total		
	Last Year	This Year	Projected	Last Year	This Year	Projected	Last Year	This Year	Projected	Last Year	This Year	Projected
I. *Environment*												
a. Macroeconomic environment												
b. Social environment												
c. Legal environment												
d. Political environment												
e. Competitive environment												
f. Overall environment												
II. *Buyers and their behavior*												
a. Number												
b. Geographic dispersion												
c. Behavior												
d. Market segments												
e. Overall buyer area												
III. *Product area*												
a. Product lines												
b. Complimentary products												
c. Substitute products												
d. Degree of innovation												
e. Growth												
f. Patterns												
g. Determinants												
h. Overall product area												

IV. *Production*
  a. Cost structure
  b. Value added
  c. Economies of scale
  d. Sources of supply
  e. Labor
  f. Level of technology
  g. Overall production area

V. *Price*
  a. Cost
  b. Competition
  c. Consumer
  d. Overall price area

VI. *Distribution*
  a. Availability
  b. Types
  c. Overall distribution area

VII. *Promotion*
  a. Advertising
  b. Personal selling
  c. Publicity
  d. Sales promotion
  e. Overall promotion area

VIII. *General overall assessment*

Figure 4–2. *General Industry Analysis*

Consideration	Company A	Company B	Company C	My Company	Relative Position
Sales and distribution					
Marketing mix capability					
Sales capability					
Channel coverage					
Strength of channel relationship					
Overall sales and distribution					
Operations and production					
Production capabilities					
Manufacturing cost position					
Overall relative costs					
Technological sophistication					
Amount of capacity					
Raw material access					
Overall operations and production					
Research and engineering					
Engineering capabilities					

Patents and copyrights
R&D ability for new products
R&D skills
Overall research and
   engineering

Financial
Cash flow
Borrowing capacity
New equity capacity
Resources
Overall financial strength

Management
Management experience
Management capabilities
   and resources
Leadership qualities of CEO
Overall management

Overall competitive company analysis

Figure 4–3. *Competitive Company Analysis*

Consideration	Company A	Company B	Company C	My Company	Relative Position
Product features					
Quality					
Convenience in using					
Utility					
Reliability					
Durability					
Expandability					
Serviceability					
Uniqueness					
Packaging					
Warranty and guarantee					
Other product features					
Overall product					
Price features					
Cost					
Mark-up					
Consumer sensitivity					
Terms of sale					
Other pricing features					
Overall price					

Distribution
  Channel coverage
  Channel relationships
  Mark-up required

Sales capability
Other distribution features
Overall distribution

Promotion features
  Promotion budget
  Advertising capability
  Personal selling capability
  Trade shows
  New product releases
  Sales promotion capability
  Other promotion features
  Overall promotion

Overall product/market analysis

Figure 4–4. *Competitive Product/Marketing Analysis*

basis, each company's capabilities in the particular industry should be evaluated in each functional area and then compared to the capabilities of your new enterprise. You should determine the best and the worst levels in each functional area. The important functional areas for evaluation include: sales and distribution, operations and production, research and engineering, financial, and general management. Again, each of these areas should be evaluated to the extent possible. For example, evaluate the management of each competitive company on an overall basis and in terms of management experience, management capabilities and resources, leadership qualities of the chief executive officer, and management's flexibility and ability to react swiftly (see figure 4–3). In addition, you should assess your management skills and those of any other company managers in these same areas. Any relative deficiencies or advantages should be recorded and corrective actions taken where necessary.

The product/market capabilities of each competitive company should similarly be analyzed in terms of each aspect of the marketing mix: product, price, distribution, and promotion (see figure 4–4). Each of these areas should also be evaluated as specifically as possible. You should compare the product features of your offering with those of competitive products or services in terms of quality, convenience in use, utility, reliability, durability, expandability, serviceability, uniqueness, packaging, and warranty and guarantee. If you find any deficiencies, note them and take corrective actions where warranted.

Evaluating the Attractiveness of the Market. Once you have a complete picture, more or less, of the particular industry and its competitive environment, you should next assess the attractiveness of the market and the strengths of your proposed new business. Base this assessment on current market conditions and try to predict conditions two years into the future. These projections can reveal some short-term phenomena and prevent some mistakes. For example, two women started a balloon delivery business, not anticipating that florists would enter the market and undercut their prices. Moreover, the nature of the business was such that other low-cost competitors entered the market easily, and within two years the market was saturated in their geographic area. So, for a new enterprise to be viable, several years of productive output are required;

products with a short-term life should be avoided. You should assess overall market attractiveness as well as market factors, competitive factors, financial/economic factors, and socio-political factors (see figure 4–5). As in the earlier figures, you should determine the important areas and obtain as much information as possible useing the marketing research process.

Assessing the Strength of Your Business. Likewise, you should assess the business strength of the new enterprise in terms of the

| Market Attractiveness Factors | Market Attractiveness | |
Product _____ Market _____	Present	2 Years Ahead
Market factors Size Growth rate Diversity (opportunity to segment) State of life cycle Demand (cylicality/seasonality) Pricing (sensitivity/stability) Distribution requirements Service requirements Level of technology Potential for functional substitution Captive customers Customer concentration Customer bargaining power		
Competitive Factors Degree of concentration Market leader's position—importance?		
Financial/economic factors Industry profitability Leveraging potential (economies of scale) Investment intensity Industry capacity utilization Barriers to entry		
Sociopolitical factors Social attitudes/trends Environmental aspects Regulatory exposure/vulnerability		
Overall market attractiveness Overall market size Probable company sales		

Figure 4–5. *Marketing and Business Form*

present and future, using the worksheet shown in figure 4–6. As always, you should be as specific as possible in the general areas of marketing, technical, production, and financial/economic, noting any strategic strengths and weaknesses, and developing a plan of action to eliminate the weaknesses. Some of the information from the competitive analysis (figures 4–3 and 4–4) will be useful in completing this worksheet.

Product _____   Market _____

	Business Strength	
	Present	2 Years Ahead

Marketing factors
  Share of served market
  Coverage
  Breadth of product line
  Product differentiation
  Product quality
  Pricing
  Sales service/effectiveness
  Distribution
  Advertising/promotion
    exposure and effectiveness)
  Company image/reputation
  Customer satisfaction		

Technical factors
  Technical service
  Patent position/technology protection
  Technology position/proprietary advantages		

Production factors
  Capability
  Cost/efficiency
  Integration/flexibility
  Available capacity/location		

Financial/economic factors
  Vertical integration
  Investment intensity
  Raw material security		

Ability to protect economics as business matures		
Overall business strength		

Figure 4–6. *Business Strength Factors*

Market Segmentation. After you have assessed the business strengths and market attractiveness, you have one final area to analyze; it is the focal point of the market plan and programs. All customers do not have the same need for a product or service. Since these needs vary, you should divide the market into groups of customers having similar needs. This process is called *market segmentation*. This area—customer analysis and segmentation—is perhaps the most vital of all.

Market segmentation can be accomplished by using six "qualitative" criteria (see table 4–3). The six qualitative segmentation criteria—demographic, geographic, psychological, benefits, volume of use, and controllable marketing elements—along with their basis in each of the three major markets—consumer, industrial, and government—should be considered carefully as you try to determine the best market segment. For example, a new business venture analyzing the market for an alarm clock that shuts off at impact against a wall—"The Wallbanger"—used demographic, geographic, psychological, and benefit segmentation. The demographic segmentation criteria considered most important were education, income, and occupation. Since the retail price for "The Wallbanger" would be around seventy-five dollars, the clock would be most attractive to consumers with at least a college education, in a business or professional occupation with an annual income above thirty thousand dollars. Geographically, target market would be concentrated in large cities. Besides having a freewheeling life-style (psychological segmentation), the targeted type of individual would enjoy the status of owning a unique clock (benefit segmentation).

Similar qualitative segmentation can be done in the industrial market. For example, a group of women entrepreneurs were deciding whether to start manufacturing specialty oils and fats used in bakeries and restaurants. The restaurants and bakeries would have to be large enough and specialized in certain products (demographic segmentation) and located in the Northeast (geographic segmentation) to make the venture successful. The target market would have to consume enough volume of the product (volume of use segmentation) and understand that the specialty oils and fats would improve the breads, cakes, pies, and other products with more efficient operations (benefit segmentation). In addition, the new company would have to have reasonable prices and service (controllable marketing element segmentation).

Table 4–3
Market Segmentation by Type of Market

Segmentation Criteria	Basis for Type of Market		
	Consumer	Industrial	Government
Demographic	Age, family size, education level, family life cyle, income, nationality, occupation, race, religion, residence, sex, social class	Number of employees, size of sales, size of profit, type of product line	Type of agency, size of budget, amount of autonomy
Geographic	Region of country, city size, market density, climate	Region of country	Federal, state, local
Psychological	Personality traits, motives, life style	Degree of industrial leadership	Degree of forward thinking
Benefits	Durability, dependability, economy, esteem enhancement, status from ownership, handiness	Dependability, reliability of seller and support service, efficiency in operation or use, enhancement of firm's earnings, durability	Dependability, reliability of seller and support services
Volume of use	Heavy, medium, light	Heavy, medium, light	Heavy, medium, light
Controllable marketing elements	Sales promotion, price, advertising, guarantee, warranty, retail store purchased service, product attributes, reputation of seller	Price, service, warranty, reputation of seller	Price, reputation of seller

You can use each of the six qualitative segmentation criteria in determining the best target market for your new business venture; the most widely used criteria, however, are demographic and geographic. This usage reflects the large amount of secondary data available, something that will be discussed later in this chapter. When determining the target market, you should remember that the numbers from market segmentation not only influence the final market plan, but also provide the basis for the sales projections in the financial plan.

Consumer analysis and market segmentation are certainly two of the most important parts of your market plan. Good market segmentation provides you with a target group of customers who are: accessible, through the firm's marketing abilities; substantial enough to make your venture profitable; and distinctive enough to be defined and defended against competitive activity.

Marketing Research Project. How can you gain information in all of these areas? Table 4–4 describes elements of a marketing research project that will help you to answer this question.

A market research project consists of five basic elements: (1) research objective and budget, (2) data availability, (3) primary research, (4) data analysis, and (5) conclusions and recommendations. The first step in any marketing research project is to establish the objectives of the research and the size of the budget. Without a clearly defined objective, the research project may not produce the information you desire. You should be careful to ensure that the information obtained is worth the cost; all too often, research budgets are larger than the value of the information warrants.

Published Data. The second step in the research project is to evaluate all available data. During the start-up phase, when there is little internal company data, you should establish a reporting system to record information in a way that will be useful in making future decisions. For example, establish a means to record customers by size of purchase, frequency of purchase, geographic location, and other relevant demographic factors, such as age, sex, and marital status, or company size and number of employees. These records will provide valuable information or customer profiles that you will find most useful in future market targeting, advertising, and distribution.

Table 4–4
Elements of a Marketing Research Project

I. Establish research objective and budget
   A. Decisions under uncertainty
   B. Budget determination

II. Data availability—secondary sources
   A. Internal
   B. External

III. Primary research
   A. Sample design
      1. Probability sampling
      2. Nonprobability sampling
   B. Research design
      1. Design selection
      2. Data collection
         a. Personal interviews
         b. Mail questionnaires
         c. Telephone survey
         d. Motivation research
         e. Retail store audits
         f. Consumer panels
         g. Focus groups
   C. Questionnaire design
      1. Questions determined
      2. Questionnaire pretested

IV. Data analysis
   A. Establishing hypothesis
   B. Nonparametric tests
   C. Parametric tests

V. Conclusions and recommendations

Many sources of external secondary data are available from federal, state, and local governments, trade associations, periodicals, and commercial services. Each of these sources should be carefully checked; because you can often obtain useful data from them without the time and costs of a primary research effort.

By far the largest single source of published data is the federal government. *The Census of Population* and *The Census of Housing* provide such information as the number of consumers by age group, income class, and sex, by geographic area. *The Census of Business* provides information on retail and wholesale sales by type of outlet by geographic area. *The Census of Manufacturing* lists industry data by geographic area. And the *County Business Patterns* indicates various types of businesses by numerous classifications. In describing industrial products, the data is classified by S.I.C. (Standard Industrial Classification) code. Each product has an S.I.C. code, a number that can be obtained from an S.I.C. code directory. For example, in developing her marketing plan, one woman entrepreneur was interested in knowing the number of firms by geographic area and S.I.C. code. By using the *Census of Business and Manufacturers, Statistical Abstract of the United States,* and the *County Business Patterns* in the business library, she obtained the needed information (as indicated in table 4–5) relatively easily. This data provided the starting point for more quantitative assessment and of course was included in her marketing plan. Other governmental agencies providing information that could be valuable are: the U.S. Patent Office, the Food and Drug Administration, the Department of Agriculture, and the Bureau of Standards. Census statistics and business information can be found in most university libraries and many public libraries.

Most major product categories have a trade association that can provide information on total product sales, distribution, and member firms. While the data is always on an aggregate basis, a discussion with the head of the association can often provide insights into the environment of the industry. Chambers of Commerce and local planning and economic development offices publish reports on businesses in their district by size and number of employees, as well as by products or services offered. These offices can be helpful to you because they are generally in a position to encourage business growth.

Periodicals are also a good source of information when you are developing your marketing plan. They can be of a general business nature: *Fortune Directory, A Guide to Consumer Markets, Market Guide, Million Dollar Directory, Middle Market Directory, Sales and Marketing Management Magazine Surveys,* and *Poor's Register of Corporations, Directors and Executives.* The periodicals can also be very product-specific, such as *Byte Magazine* and *Computer Age.* Checking the periodicals for information before you prepare the marketing plan is a good idea. For example, one woman entrereneur used the information from the *Survey of Buying Power of*

Table 4–5
Number of Firms by Geographic Area and S.I.C.

S.I.C.	New England	Middle Atlantic	East North Central	West North Central
Retail	107,200	300,500	320,900	158,500
Wholesale	18,577	69,469	68,175	41,111
Manufacturing	24,286	76,422	63,062	20,623
Services	110,900	307,700	311,100	153,200
Mining	323	2,320	3,334	2,532
Construction	6,388	13,244	16,562	11,653

Sources: *Census of Business and Manufactures, Statistical Abstract of the United States,* and *County Business Patterns.*

Sales and Marketing Management Magazine as an integral part of her market evaluation (see table 4–6).

A final source of published information is commercial services. This information involves varying costs, depending on the amount and type of information you want. These services include: *Nielsen Retail Index, Audits and Surveys, National Total Market Index, MRCA Consumer Panels, Simmons Media/Marketing Service*, and *National Family Opinion*. Again, given the costs of these services, you should check other sources of information first.

A good marketing plan will contain information from at least one source. Not only is the information valuable in its own right, it also demonstrates to outside individuals evaluating your plan that you have done your homework and know the market.

Primary Research. Once you have obtained secondary data, you can tailor it to your specific objective through primary research— the collection of original data. This third part of a research project can be as broad or narrow as you need, depending on the time and money available. As table 4–4 indicates, primary research has three major components: sample design, research design, and question- naire design. Entire books have been written on this topic, so we shall simply focus here on the greatest problem area—question- naire design.

There are many questioning techniques available to you. Types, with their advantages and disadvantages, and examples of each are shown in table 4–7. Every woman entrepreneur's business plan should

South Atlantic	East South Central	West South Central	Mountain	Pacific
294,000	121,700	202,500	96,000	253,700
49,836	20,630	39,537	17,059	45,397
37,961	15,746	21,883	8,679	42,433
273,500	92,700	180,900	100,100	304,100
3,400	3,133	10,583	3,852	1,824
22,112	6,346	9,038	6,679	14,677

contain and reflect some primary research on at least a small-scale pilot project basis, so you should be careful to design questions that are relevant, easily understood, and quantifiable. Including a primary research project in a marketing plan, regardless of its size, demonstrates effort and increases the plan's credibility to possible sources of capital, and provides valuable, relevant information for your final marketing program.

Data Analysis, Conclusions, and Recommendations. The last two parts of the marketing research project—data analysis, and conclusions and recommendations—involve analyzing the data and evaluating the results in a meaningful way. The methodology used in evaluation is important, but perhaps equally important is the manner in which the data are displayed. Tables, charts, and figures add credibility to the business plan as they display the data in a way helpful in making managerial decisions. Of course, no research project is worth the cost if appropriate conclusions and recommendations do not result that give direction to the final marketing program. Indeed, the marketing research information can give you the tools to assess quantitatively the market, as well as the internal and external environments confronting you. As figure 4–7 demonstrates, these concerns are an integral part of the market plan, with the internal and external environments providing the framework and the market the focal point of the actual market plan that you will use to gain sales for the new enterprise.

Marketing Mix. The actual market plan itself is composed of four elements—the product mix, price mix, distribution mix, and promo-

Table 4-6
Sample Summary of Sales & Marketing Management Magazine's Projections by Region and State

Region/State	Population					Effective Buying Income				Retail Sales				Buying Power Index	
	Total Pop. 12/31/83 (Thous)	Total Pop. 12/31/88 (Thous)	% Change 1983–1988	Total Households 12/31/88 (Thous)	% Change 1983–1988	Total EBI 1988 ($000)	% Change 1983–1988	Average Household EBI 1983	Average Household EBI 1988	Total Retail Sales 1988 ($000)	% Change 1983–1988	Retail Sales Per Household 1983	Retail Sales Per Household 1988	1983	1988
East North Central	41,700.3	42,068.3	.9	15,715.2	3.7	640,944,471	55.1	27,270	40,785	302,800,037	51.9	13,161	19,268	17.4524	16.8268
Illinois	11,511.2	11,605.7	.8	4,398.1	4.0	190,650,908	54.9	29,113	43,348	85,834,959	52.1	13,346	19,516	5.0462	4.8648
Indiana	5,526.3	5,611.9	1.5	2,019.1	3.0	76,988,783	55.3	25,273	38,130	40,542,194	53.0	13,511	20,079	2.2033	2.1326
Michigan	9,129.3	9,161.7	.4	3,324.7	2.9	139,500,468	54.1	28,023	41,959	67,046,475	50.1	13,825	20,166	3.8476	3.6810
Ohio	10,767.4	10,807.7	.4	4,138.5	3.6	160,575,634	55.1	25,906	38,800	76,963,251	51.6	12,702	18,597	4.4198	4.2548
Wisconsin	4,766.1	4,881.3	2.4	1,834.8	5.7	73,228,678	57.5	26,776	39,911	32,413,158	53.8	12,133	17,666	1.9355	1.8936

Source: Adapted from *Sales & Marketing Management Magazine*, Copyright October 29, 1984; Survey of Buying Power, Il.

tion mix. These are the controllable marketing elements of the new enterprise that you can use to satisfy the customer and sell the firm's offering; and this is often referred to as a marketing mix. Figure 4–8 shows that the marketing mix has its own mix of options that must be put together in a total package to satisfy the customer. When developing this approach, you need to remember that the customer buys a total package, not just the product, the price, or the distribution.

Product/Service Mix. In composing the best product mix, you will be making many decisions on the physical product itself—its quality, the assortment of different features, the variety of products to be offered, the breadth and depth of the line, and so on. In some instances, colors, taste, fragrance, style, and fashion will be involved. The physical product must also be packaged for protection and display, placed under the appropriate warranty and quarantee, and, if applicable, serviced properly.

If you are planning to offer a service, you must establish the service mix. You must make decisions regarding hours of service availability, amount of personal selling and follow up, parking and accessibility, and mix of services offered at the business.

Price Mix. Closely tied to these decisions regarding the product is the price. The price has its own mix of determinants—cost, competition, and the consumer. No other variable in the marketing mix is so little understood and yet so important as price. Cost establishes the floor below which the price cannot drop, at least over the long run, in order for profit to be made. Competition establishes the boundaries for the price of the product, because consumers are accustomed to established price ranges for a particular product category. Needless to say, the consumer ultimately decides whether the price established is correct, for how the consumer evaluates the price and the rest of your marketing mix in relation to that of competitive offerings determines whether he will buy your product or someone else's.

Distribution Mix. Like the price mix, the distribution mix is little understood by most organizations, particularly when it comes to the channels of distribution aspect of the mix. The distribution mix is composed of channels of distribution and physical distribution. Deciding on channels of distribution means determining which of the many retailers, wholesalers, and representatives (if any) should be used to connect the organization and the consumer by making the product available to the consumer. The second aspect of the distribution mix, physical distribution, is the process of physically moving

Table 4–7
Examples of Questioning Techniques

Questioning Techniques	Example	Advantages	Disadvantages
Dichotomous questions	Do you usually like to try a new store? ___ Yes ___ No	1. Easy to answer 2. Can be used to screen before asking further questions 3. Easy to tabulate 4. Provides a definite answer	1. Forces a choice 2. Provides no detailed information
Multiple choice questions	If you were going to buy a car, which of the following makes would you buy? ___ Car A ___ Car B ___ Car C ___ Car D	1. Usually avoids forcing an arbitrary choice 2. Easy to answer 3. Easy to tabulate	1. Choices may not be all-encompassing 2. Choices may not be totally distinctive
Preference	Which of these stores do you prefer? ___ Store A ___ Store B ___ Store C ___ Store D	1. Gives information on preference 2. Easy to respond	1. Prefrence may not reflect purchase choice 2. Choice may present some confusion
Rating	On a scale from one to seven (with 1 being disliked very much and	1. Gives important information on relative feelings about various product attributes	1. Distinctions on scale may not be clear to respondent 2. Provides scale graduations that

	Advantages	Disadvantages
7 being liked very much) indicate your overall feeling about the overall store by circling the number that corresponds to your opinion.	2. Does not force an arbitrary choice 3. Provides a wide range of responses for comparative purposes	may not be commensurate with knowledge of respondent
Ranking Rank in order from one to five (with 1 being the best and 5 the worst) your opinion of the following stores: —— Store A —— Store B —— Store C —— Store D —— Store E	1. Provides valuable information on relative consumer opinions on products or attributes 2. Provides a definite answer 3. Yields information quickly	1. Is probably the most confusing type of question for the consumer to answer 2. Provides no information on how good the best product is 3. Provides no information on relative differences between ranks of products
Open-ended questions Why do you shop at this particular store?	1. Does not bias respondent's response with established answers 2. Provides a wide range of information 3. Provides information of more depth	1. Interpretation of answer requires time and may vary between interpretors 2. Difficult to tabulate

Source: This table is an adapted version of one in Robert D. Hisrich and Michael P. Peters, *Marketing a New Product: Its Planning, Development, and Control* (Menlo Park, Calif.: The Benjamin/Cummings Publishing Co., 1978), 99–100.

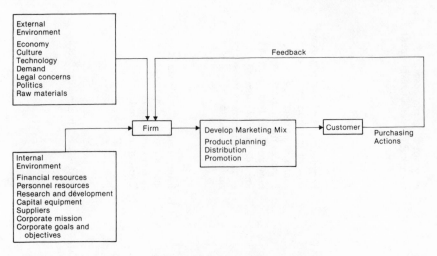

Source: Robert D. Hisrich and Michael P. Peters, *Marketing Decisions for New and Mature Products* (Columbus, Ohio: Charles E. Merrill Publishing Co., 1984), 77.

Figure 4–7. *Marketing Planning System*

the product to the consumer through storage, inventory, transportation, and warehousing.

Promotion Mix. The final part of the marketing mix has more continuous impact on every individual each day and moreover, receives the most criticism—promotion. Promotion includes five components: advertising, personal selling, publicity, public relations, and sales promotion. The first two—advertising and personal selling—are the most familiar aspects of marketing, and they receive the largest amount of marketing expenditures. Advertising, a paid, nonpersonal presentation, confronts consumers with, for example, entreaties to buy Nike running shoes in the morning sports section of the newspaper and encouragement to drink Budweiser beer on the Johnny Carson television show. Personal selling, paid, personal presentation, mainly involves the sale of products from one company to another company, like when a Procter and Gamble salesperson asks a store manager of a Kroger supermarket to feature Duncan Hines cake mix in an in-store promotion. Personal selling also involves the sale of products from a firm to a consumer. Publicity and public relations is probably the fastest growing area in the promotion mix. Firms are becoming increasingly concerned that a proper

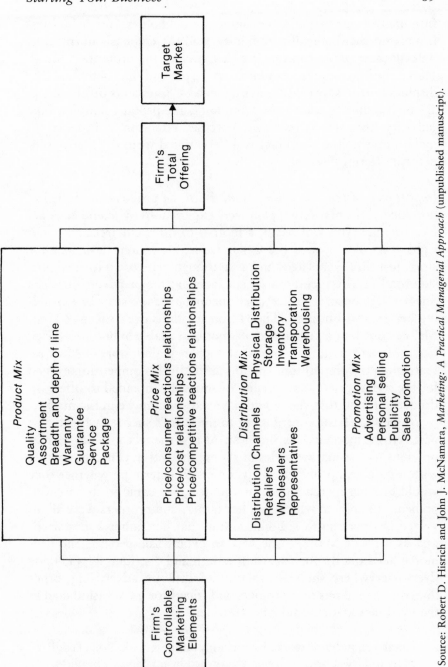

Figure 4–8. *Marketing Activities*

Source: Robert D. Hisrich and John J. McNamara, *Marketing: A Practical Managerial Approach* (unpublished manuscript).

firm image be presented to consumers, stockholders, other business firms, and the financial community, and the emphasis in this area will continue in the future. The final area of the promotion mix— sales promotion—involves nonrecurring promotional activities, like displays in stores, price-off packs, (such as "four cents off this package of cake mix"), trade shows and fairs, and product samples. Like publicity, this area is receiving increased attention as firms try to make sure that their product is differentiated from the many competitive offerings available.

Importance of the Marketing Plan. Both the problems and the importance of the marketing plan were experienced by Jeanie Ferrone. Ms. Ferrone, you will recall, a mother of three children, all under eight years old, opened the Cellar Door, a discount designer shoe store, just three years ago, and even though her store is located on a side road in a residential area and does no major advertising, she does enough business to consider opening a second store or expanding her present business. The reason for the store's success? First, Ms. Ferrone had a keen sense of what is available in her area (Cape Cod, Massachusetts) in terms of higher-quality stores. After researching the competition, she found that little competition existed for the styles, prices, and quality of shoes she intended to offer. Indeed, she found that she would have a distinct niche in the market.

A second factor contributing to the store's success was the way Ms. Ferrone marketed her business. At first she relied on her friends' opinions to test-market styles of shoes. She was in constant contact with a core group of typical customers to determine whether they would buy her merchandise. In addition, she came from an entrepreneurial family in which she, her father, and brothers were all involved in operating a regional airline that her father had started, and as a result Ms. Ferrone was an expert salesperson. She promoted her store through word of mouth and distributed handmade flyers everywhere she went. She relied little on advertising, other than direct mailings to customers and friends or an occasional ad in the local newspaper. Said Ms. Ferrone:

> I think of how hard I worked to make my business work. Why, I used to fly to New York, borrow a van owned by my family's business,

and drive to a New Jersey showroom. After selecting my shoes, I'd load them from the warehouse into the van and fly them home the same day so I could sell them next day. Somehow I survived. In the beginning, I had no sales quotas or systems for revenue projections. It was sort of hit-or-miss until I realized that I was making money and had better keep these things straight.

The Financial Plan

The sales projections from the marketing plan are the first and most important element in the financial plan, another problem area for most women entrepreneurs. Nancy Highet was no exception.

Ms. Highet is co-owner of NH Designs in New York City. Her three-year-old business designs and imports cotton and wool rag rugs that will soon be distributed nationally. Ms. Highet had an extensive background in interior decorating, which sharpened her people skills and her ability to sell ideas. Nevertheless, she was intimidated initially by the financial side of making her new business run. Her solution was to confront the problem:

> If you're afraid of math and numbers, the only way to overcome this is to meet the problem head-on. Get involved and learn about payables and receivables. It is important to make decisions based on a good financial understanding of your business's capabilities rather than on the emotional or artistic aspects.

Like Ms. Highet, most women entrepreneurs lack experience in finance and therefore consider it their weakest business skill. This lack of experience and confidence in negotiating financial matters leaves potential lenders doubtful about whether the business will succeed. Experience and confidence in dealing with money, plus a well-organized business plan with clearly defined goals and objectives, are musts for a woman entrepreneur seeking outside capital. To overcome this weakness, you should become familiar with the basic concepts of simple economics, profit and loss statements, and how to apply for a loan.

While the extent of the financial plan varies depending on the nature of the business, whether it is a one-person, cash-only service business or a high-technology export business, every new venture needs one. If the only outcome of the financial plan is to prevent you as you start a new enterprise from working for poverty wages or less, then it has been useful. Several parts of the financial plan are important: sources and uses of funds, break-even analysis, income statement, balance sheet, and cash flow.

Sources and Applications of Funds Statement. One key question that anyone investing in a business asks is, "What is the money going to be used for?" A good method for answering this question is to use a modified version of the sources and applications of funds statement presented in figure 4–9. This is probably one of the easiest financial statements to prepare, and yet it will provide you with a succinct statement of where the money will come from—loans, personal savings, or other sources. The bottom part of the statement indicates how the money will be used—buildings, equipment, renovations, or working capital. When you are buying equipment, you should also prepare a capital equipment list similar to the one in figure 4–10.

Income Statement. Two other financial documents can help you to assess both the profitability of the venture and how the resources

Sources

Bank loans:
   1. Mortgage loan $ _____
   2. Term loan $ _____
   3. Reserved loan $ _____
Other _____ $ _____

Total $ _____

Applications

Purchase building $ _____
Equipment $ _____
Renovations $ _____
Inventory $ _____
Working capital $ _____
Reserve for contingencies $ _____
Other _____ $ _____

Total $ _____

Figure 4–9. *Sources and Applications of Funds*

	Model	Cost or List Price
Major equipment and normal accessories		$
_____	_____	_____
_____	_____	_____
_____	_____	_____
_____	_____	_____
_____	_____	_____
	Total	$
Minor shop equipment		$
_____	_____	_____
_____	_____	_____
_____	_____	_____
	Total	$
Other equipment		$
_____	_____	_____
_____	_____	_____
_____	_____	_____
	Total	$
	Total	$

Figure 4–10. *Capital Equipment List*

will be allocated. The most important of these is the income statement, which is sometimes called the profit and loss (P & L) statement. As the name suggests, the profit and loss statement indicates the revenues and expenses of an enterprise and its resulting profit or loss for a particular period of time. When this period of time is in the future, as is the case for a venture just starting out, the statements are called *pro forma income statements*, examples of which are indicated in appendix III, tables A–D. These pro forma statements are so important for the profitability of the new enterprise at start-up and in the future that they should be done: on a three-year summary basis (table A), by month for the first year (table B), by quarter for the second year (table C), and by quarter for the third year (table D). Except for the time period covered, each statement is basically the same. The sales figure (the most important and difficult part) comes from the marketing plan discussed earlier in this chapter. This sales figure is so critical that a brief justification for it, with reference to appropriate aspects of the marketing plan, should be indicated at the bottom of the statement. From this sales figure subtract the cost of making the product (cost of goods sold) to arrive at the all-important gross profit figure. This figure minus the operating expenses gives you the pretax profit or loss of the new venture. The operating expenses can include such items as outside labor, operating supplies, salaries, wages and commissions, repairs and maintenance, advertising and promotion, bad debts, rent, utilities, and insurance. The exact nature of the operating expenses depend on the nature of your business venture.

Although it may sound strange, you should not be concerned when a loss instead of a profit appears in the first year. In fact, in realistic terms you should perhaps be more concerned if the first year results in a profit, as this may indicate an error in some figures. Most new ventures do not show a profit in the first year, and many do not until the third or even fourth year. A longer period to make a profit is more typical of high technology and manufacturing ventures. This two- to four-year time period for a new enterprise to achieve profits is so well accepted that some individuals will examine figures that show a profit in year one even more thoroughly than those that show a loss before deciding on a financial commitment.

Once you have calculated the figures for the first year on the pro forma income statements, you will find that the statements for the next two years are easier. The expenses of year one as a percent of sales are used as a percentage of the higher sales levels of future years. There may be a learning curve, or improved performance resulting from experience, so that future expenses as a percentage of sales will be lower. This often takes place in the cost-goods-sold category, reflecting both increasing efficiencies in production and decreasing costs of materials as larger quantities are purchased.

Balance Sheet. The third important type of statement in the financial plan—the balance sheet—presents a picture of the accounting value of the enterprise at a particular point in time. While not as important as the pro forma income statements, the pro forma balance sheet (see figure 4–11) gives data for further evaluation of the business. The balance sheet is composed of three major sections:

Assets

Current assets

Cash $ ___
Accounts receivable (net) ___
Merchandise inventory ___
Supplies ___
Prepaid expenses ___
Total current assets $ ___

Fixed assets

Fixtures $ ___
Vehicles ___
Equipment ___
Leasehold improve-ments ___
Building ___
Land ___
Total fixed assets $ ___

Total assets $ ___

Liabilities and Net Worth

Current liabilities

Accounts payable $ ___
Other ___
Total current liabilities $ ___

Long-term liabilities

Notes payable (a) ___
Bank loan payable (b) ___
Other loans payable (c) ___
Total long-term liabilities $ ___

Total liabilities $ ___

Net worth: Owner's equity $ ___

Total liabilities and net worth $ ___

1. Accounts payable (name of account):

   1. _____ $ ___
   2. _____ $ ___
   3. _____ $ ___

2. Liabilities (name of lender):

   (a) _____ $ ___
   (b) _____ $ ___
   (c) _____ $ ___

Figure 4–11. *Balance Sheet*

(1) total assets, which comprise current and fixed assets, (2) total liabilities, which comprise both current and long-term liabilities, and (3) net worth. Each of these sections has its own subdivisions, depending on the nature of the business. For example, current assets are composed of cash, accounts receivable, merchandise inventory, supplies, and prepaid expenses. Of these areas, the greatest source of problems for the new enterprise is usually cash, or more specifically, the lack of cash. This lack is so important that you should undertake a separate analysis—a pro forma cash flow analysis.

Cash Flow. The concept of cash flow is as straightforward and basic in business as it is in your personal finances. Cash receipts result in a cash increase, and cash disbursements result in a cash decrease. The combined results constitute the cash flow.

An estimate of future cash flows is very important at the start-up phase of a new venture, and should be done on a monthly basis for the first year and on a quarterly basis for the second and third years, using a tailored version of tables E–H, appendix III. As was the case with the pro forma income statements, a three-year summary should also be compiled. This estimate of cash flow is the key to survival for the new venture, as it indicates whether or not cash receipts are building up relatively faster than cash disbursements. A frequent cause of failure for new businesses is that fast growth can produce a cash shortage that cannot be covered. To ensure that this does not happen to you, develop the pro forma cash flows very carefully, using all the resources available.

Break-even Analysis. Another useful tool for financial analysis is break-even analysis. Break-even analysis takes into account fixed and variable costs and then indicates the number of units that must be sold for total revenue (sales times price) to equal total costs. This point, the break-even point, can be determined by using the formulas in figure 4–12. Once you have determined the break-even point, compare it with the projected sales, taking into account the total size of the market and the new enterprise's realistic share of the market. This analysis can help you avoid such errors as lacking enough production capacity just to break even, or needing to achieve a 50 percent share of the total market in order to reach break-even sales.

Sales $ _____
Cost of goods sold $ _____
Gross profit $ _____
Fixed expenses $ _____

Step 1: Divide gross profit by sales to show percentage relationship.

$$\frac{\text{gross profit}}{\text{sales}} = \text{gross profit as \% of sales}$$

Step 2: Divide fixed expenses by gross profit as % of sales expressed as a decimal.

$$\frac{\text{fixed expenses}}{\text{gross profit}} = \text{break-even}$$

Figure 4–12. *Break-even Analysis*

Test of Financial Reality. A final helpful tool to help you determine the sales volume needed to meet the income requirements is indicated in figure 4–13. This quick test of financial reality is a useful addition to the break-even analysis, indicating as it does the sales volume needed to produce a sufficient income rather than merely the break-even point. The critical areas that you will have to examine in calculating the income-producing sales volume are: the wage the business should provide; the rate of return used on the money invested in the business; and the size of the reinvestment needs of the business. Regardless of the final numbers used in each of these areas, this calculation will indicate to you the sales volume needed to compensate you for your time and at the same time provide a fair return on the financial investment in the new business.

Importance of the Financial Plan. Each of these financial analyses will indicate the financial health of the new enterprise and will also help in gaining any outside financial support (the specific issues involved in obtaining a bank loan will be treated separately, in the first section of chapter 5). Indeed, a good financial plan is vital to the new enterprise, but it is an area in which too often women entrepreneurs have little if any experience.

Libbie Agran, however, is one woman entrepreneur who recognizes the importance of strength in finance. She has been running financial-planning seminars for women in Los Angeles for six years.

I. Type of business: _____

II. Income requirements of business:

   A. Wage projection:

     (1) What is your current annual salary? _____

     (2) What's the standard owner's
     salary for this type of business? _____

     (3) What are your annual income
     needs? _____

     (4) Sum of 1 + 2 + 3 _____

     (5) Divide line 4   (____) =
     by the number 3.   3 _____

     (6) What % of your time and/or
     income will be tied to this
     business? _____

     (7) Wage requirements of business:
       (A6) × (A5) = ( ) × ( ) = _____

   B. Investment income:

     (1) How much of your money will you
     invest in this business? _____

     (2) What rate of return can you get
     on this money now? (If you don't
     know, put in the current bank
     certificate of deposit rate.) _____

     (3) Return on investment
     requirements:
       (B2) × (B1) = ( ) × ( ) = _____

   C. Reinvestment needs of business:
   How much of the business's profits must be
   annually retained for investment in new equipment
   and expansion of inventory and accounts receivable? _____

III. Total income requirements of business
    (A + B + C): _____

IV. Projected profits as a percent of sales. _____

   V. Sales necessary to meet income requirements:

$$\frac{III}{IV} = \left(\frac{\underline{\qquad}}{(\quad)}\right) = \underline{\qquad}$$

Source: Carl Schweser, "A Quick Test of Financial Reality for Would-Be Entrepreneurs,"
Journal of Small Business Management (October 1982):80.

Figure 4–13. *Quick Test of Financial Reality*

Her seminars teach women skills in personal finance and bolster confidence in this area. With experience as a business manager and a graduate degree in business administration, Ms. Agran has decided to be selective about clients and to limit the business to what it does best.

The Organizational Plan

The final part of the business plan is the organizational plan. It addressees two key matters: the capability of the management team and the legal form of the business.

The Management Team and the Form of the Business. The capability of the management team plays a vitally important part in determining the success of the new enterprise. At start-up, this "team" may just be the entrepreneur herself, but as the business starts to grow, other managers will be added. The capabilities of each member of the management team should be thoroughly discussed in the business plan and a detailed resumé of each attached as an appendix. You should include the past accomplishments of each individual and indicate how these will be useful in helping to ensure the new business's success. Particularly important in a management team member is any previous experience in similar business situations.

When the management team includes more than one person, you will need to develop an organization chart. This chart should indicate who does what and who is responsible to whom. Clear lines of communication and responsibility should be delineated to ensure that all the critical decisions can be made without any confusion or problems. One woman entrepreneur offers advice in this area:

> When my partner and I started our business, there were no clear definitions of responsibility; we both did everything. This worked fine for about two months, until problems arose because our employees were unclear as to which owner's instructions they should follow. We finally agreed to divide up our responsibilities, each taking on those areas we felt strongest in.

You should also establish a compensation plan that reflects the abilities and value of the individuals involved. Salaries in the business plan should reflect true market salaries, not lower ones. If these salaries cannot be met during the early years of operation, this should be remedied as soon as the business can afford to.

Finally, a board of directors should be designated. A good board of directors is composed of individuals who possess skills valuable to the success of the new enterprise, such as marketing, law, accounting, and finance. Having a banker on the board is a particularly good idea, for a banker can provide easier access to loans in the future. The presence of a banker also lends an aura of credibility and longevity to a start-up company.

In addition to the management side of the organization, you need to decide on the legal organizational form of the new enterprise. This decision will influence (or be influenced by) such matters as costs of set-up, liability, accountability and autonomy of the entrepreneur, taxes, and sources of capital. Determining the general organizational structure involves two primary decisions: whether to be profit or nonprofit, and corporate or noncorporate. Within each of these general classifications there are many options, and you may find the advice of a lawyer necessary in deciding on the initial form of the organization. General guidelines for selecting a lawyer are described in the next chapter, so a word of caution will suffice here. Many new ventures have failed because too much money was spent on legal fees to establish an optimum organizational structure and to receive patent protection, but while such things may be good for the enterprise, until a product is sold the company has no source of revenue. So, since the initial organizational structure is often modified as the new venture grows and matures, you should not put too much time, money, and effort into the initial formation.

Deciding How to Organize. Nonprofit ventures can be either corporate or noncorporate, but most are noncorporate. A venture is given nonprofit status only when any profits, with the exception of reasonable overhead and salaries dependent on services rendered, are put back into the corporation to benefit a particular segment of society. Traditional nonprofit organizations can be classified in the general categories of charitable, cooperative commerce, cultural, political, and social, with many different types under each classification. For example, there are many different types of charitable nonprofit organizations; some are involved in civic affairs, some educational, some health, and some in the area of religion.

Recently the nonprofit corporation has become the most popular organizational structure for nonprofit enterprises. This nonprofit corporation is a legal entity of its own with the corresponding limited liability, and as such, it can negotiate contracts, buy and sell property, and solicit funds.

There are of course several advantages to establishing a nonprofit organization. These advantages include cheaper postal rates, tax deductibility for individuals donating to the organization, exemption from having to contribute to certain unemployment funds, and by far the most important, exemption from real estate and other forms of taxation.

On the other hand, there are disadvantages to establishing a nonprofit organization. Nonprofit organizations are scrutinized by government agencies like the IRS and by the general public to ensure that all expenses are in line and there is no excess profitability. Also, your salary in a nonprofit organization is carefully monitored and controlled and cannot increase dramatically with an increase in the profits of the business.

So, if one of your purposes is to make money, then you should establish a profit organization. It can take one of three basic forms: sole proprietorship, partnership, or corporation.[7] Each of these basic forms has a number of variations.

Sole Proprietorship. A sole proprietorship is what the name suggests—an individual conducting an unincorporated business for profit. Since this is the easiest and most inexpensive way to start a new enterprise, it is frequently used by women entrepreneurs, particularly in small service industries. The only legal requirement in establishing a sole proprietorship is that you register the name of the business as the local laws specify. Any profits accrue directly to the proprietor, who is of course the undisputed head of the enterprise. There are, however, two major disadvantages of a sole proprietorship. First, all profits are taxed at the personal income tax rate, not the lower corporate rate. Second, you are personally liable for all business debts and injuries. This problem may seem quite serious, but for many businesses the possibility of any significant liability claim is very low and can be protected through insurance. In spite of these two disadvantages, unless there is a significant amount of capital involved, sole proprietorships are probably the best way to start a new enterprise. If you like, you can change the organizational form later once sales and profits have been established.

Partnership. Some woman entrepreneurs start their new ventures as partnerships. While there are several types of specific partnership arrangements available to suit the particular business situation, the one most commonly used is the general partnership. This type of organizational structure is an extension of a sole proprietorship in which two or more individuals become a legal entity—a business—for all transactional purposes. The partnership is viewed by the Internal Revenue Service as a tax-reporting but not a tax-paying entity. Each individual in the partnership pays personal taxes on the amount of profits personally accrued. It is true that a general partnership allows the partners to share administrative responsibilities and decision making and in this way it may be useful in the start-up phase of the business, but few if any partnerships survive over the life of the enterprise. While compatibility may initially exist between the partners, it rarely lasts, since very often one of the strongest motives for a woman entrepreneur's starting a business is independence. Moreover, partnerships must be based on the business rather than on friendship. So, unless the partners are very *sympatico* and the partnership agreement is carefully worked out to ensure that this need for independence is met, the partnership will probably be short lived.

Although a partnership can actually be started without a legal partnership agreement, doing so is generally ill-advised. Regardless of the length or complexity of the partnership agreement, it should be written down on paper before money starts to flow or liabilities occur. Even among the closest friends or relatives, money and liabilities can cause major misunderstandings unless agreements about them have already been established *in writing* before the event. This principle cannot be stressed enough. A general partnership agreement should cover (at the very least): the responsibilities of each partner, the investment required by each partner, provisions for partnership withdrawal, the admission of new partners, the formula for distributing the profits, and the duration of the partnership.

There are four commonly used variations of this general partnership agreement. The first is a regular partnership where both parties own the business equally. The second is a limited partnership. It is composed of one general partner—the woman entrepreneur—who actively manages and is personally liable for the obligations of the enterprise, and a number of limited partners who do not take any management role but are the financial backers. In this arrangement all partners are clearly disclosed; this being the difference between a limited partnership and a silent partnership. In a silent partnership, one or more of the financial backers (the limited partners) remain anonymous. The final type of partnership arrangement is a joint-stock company. These were once frequently used as a hybrid between a partnership and a corporation, but once the corporate laws became solidified in the United States, the advantages of the joint-stock company began to disappear.

Corporation. A corporation differs from the noncorporate form of business structures in that it is viewed as a legal entity for purposes of taxation, liability, and employee benefits. Corporate profits are taxed at a lower rate than those of individuals who are earning the same amount of income. In this case, however, a kind of double taxation occurs in that any income taken out of the corporation by the woman entrepreneur is also taxed at her personal income tax rate.

Next, and perhaps most important, the corporation is responsible for any debts, injuries due to product or company negligence, and any other legal liabilities. Investors (shareholders) may not be sued. For this reason many ventures start as corporations, since without the corporate status (and the accompanying lack of personal liability) it might not be possible to find any investors.

Finally, some employee benefits related to retirement, such as larger contributions to Keogh and workman's compensation, are available under the corporate structure, but not under the noncorporate structure. These employee benefits are becoming fewer and fewer in number, however, and in fact can usually be replaced through a program available from an insurance company. Such additional benefits are not a reason for you to incorporate.

In addition to double taxation, there are some other negative benefits in incorporating the new venture. First, greater initial expense is involved in establishing a corporation. Not only are there more legal fees, but there are also more fees required for filing to obtain corporate status. These fees reflect yet another disadvantage of a corporate structure—significant amounts of paperwork are required to satisfy federal and state laws for obtaining corporate status.

Filling out forms will not only cost you more money but also costs a very important commodity of which you never have enough at this stage of the new enterprise—time.

Finally, a corporate structure does place a damper on one of the motivations of the woman entrepreneur for starting her own business—independence. A corporation must have a board of directors elected by the investors (stockholders) who in turn set policy that is then implemented by you and by other corporate managers. Although this is the procedure, in reality the board of directors usually offers sound advice and does not interfere with the entrepreneur's actions unless there are good business reasons for doing so.

It should be apparent by now that you should carefully consider the advantages and disadvantages of setting up a corporation. Unless liability from anyone sustaining personal injury is possible, you will probably want to start a new enterprise as a sole proprietorship or a partnership (regular, limited, or silent), unless of course your potential investors think otherwise. These noncorporate structures work particularly well for service industries, in which most women entrepreneurs establish businesses and which involve limited initial capital, plant, and equipment. The initial noncorporate structure can always be changed to a corporate one when sales, profits, investment, and liability warrant doing so.

Once your business is thriving you may well wish to incorporate, in which case you should know more about corporate structures. There are two general types of corporations—regular and Subchapter S—each of which has numerous variations. The regular corporation is the better-known corporate structure, the one that most women entrepreneurs think of when starting their ventures. This type of corporation requires several procedures: obtaining a corporate taxpayer identification number from the IRS; obtaining an approval from the secretary of the state in which you are incorporating by filing a certificate of incorporation; and holding a stockholders' meeting to elect directors who in turn elect the corporate officers. The directors of each corporation must then meet at least once each year thereafter, keeping the minutes of the meeting on record. Obviously the process, particularly the filing of the certificate of incorporation, is difficult and time consuming; it also varies from one state to the next. Many women entrepreneurs who incorporate do so in the state of Delaware because of its corporate laws, which are less stringent.[8]

A corporation is either publicly held or closely held, depending on the type of stockholders. A closely held corporation is generally one where all the stock is owned by persons (or members of their immediate family) who are actively involved in the management of the business. Though less frequently employed than the publicly held corporation, this kind of corporate structure provides the liability protection, the benefits of being incorporated, and the absence of the public scrutiny applied to a partnership. Since the laws and restrictions again vary from state to state, you should consult an attorney who knows the laws affecting closely held corporations in the various states.

Another form of corporation is the Subchapter S corporation, which is now just called an S corporation.[9] There are certain benefits and restrictions to an S corporation that result from a modification of the original 1958 conception in the Small Business Tax Reform Act. To qualify, a new venture has to have no more than thirty-five shareholders and no more than 20 percent of its income earned from passive investments. The losses of the corporation can be deducted by the individual stockholders and can be earned forward (or backward) to offset any gains; this is a significant advantage in attracting capital from individual investors who want a tax write-off the first several years when the corporation is losing money. When the new venture starts to earn a profit, the structure can be changed from an S corporation to a regular corporation with its accompanying tax laws. However, before deciding on an S corporation, you should definitely consult a lawyer who is familiar with the tax and other benefits of your particular state, for states vary widely in their treatment of these matters.

Importance of the Organizational Plan. Regardless of the structure or the organizational plan, you should make sure that the final form best accomplishes the objectives of the enterprise and is revised as needed. The importance of this part of the business plan for the success of the new venture is evident in the case of Carol Dodd.

Carol Dodd started Martha's Deli and Cheese Shop in 1971 in a small, rented store with only three thousand dollars and one employee. It was the first store on the island of Martha's Vineyard to offer fresh bagels, cheese, and coffee by the pound. Eventually the business evolved into a deli offering croissants, quiche, soups, and sandwiches, and then into a full-fledged restaurant offering three meals a day. Her revenues went from $17,000 the first year to more than $410,000 in the tenth year. As the business grew, Ms. Dodd had the opportunity to remain a sole proprietor, incorporate, or take on a partner. She chose to remain a sole proprietor until the seventh year of operation, when she brought a minority partner (with less than equal ownership) into the business. She offers the following advice on partnerships:

> Friendship is not the best basis on which to take on a partner. Be sure that you both understand it is a business arrangement and that everything is clearly spelled out.

Another important part of Ms. Dodd's success was her willingness to work hard and adapt organizational policies and responsibilities when necessary. During the ten years of operation she was constantly remodeling and expanding services, which meant also modifying policies and duties constantly:

> I started off with just a baker. Then I realized I needed front counter help to sell goods, and finally I decided I needed waitresses. I performed nearly every job myself in the beginning to determine what needed to be done. That made it easier to delegate the responsibilities. Basically, these things just needed to be done so we did them, and our policies evolved from this process.

Her personnel policies were very good, and most employees returned year after year. What made Ms. Dodd a successful woman entrepreneur? She offers this advice:

> Believe that you can do it. You don't have to have all the education in the world, but you do need guts, instinct, and determination. You can't be afraid to get your hands dirty if you're going to make it.

5
Early Operations
of the New Venture

It would be nice to have financing available based on one's own background—not on one's husband's income.

It is difficult to determine how to hire experts. Women often need guidance on the questions to ask accountants, lawyers, and market research firms. The advice of experts should be sought early in the operations of the business.

These quotes from three women entrepreneurs reflect important issues in the early operations of the new enterprise. Women entrepreneurs frequently ask: "How do I determine my strengths and weaknesses in running a business? How do I hire experts in areas where I am weak?" And perhaps the most frequently asked question: "How do I obtain a bank loan?" One woman entrepreneur, Marion Snyder, encountered these problems in the early operations of her business.

Ms. Snyder believes that future entrepreneurs should take practical business courses on such subjects as taxes, leases, and networking. She believes that understanding the real world is essential for women to become confident as business owners.

Ms. Snyder is a good judge of what you need to know. She recently started her third successful entrepreneurial venture, MAIL-BOX, a private post office providing answering services, Telex, copy services, and mailing addresses for small business owners in Washington, D.C. Her previous venture involved converting old gas stations into self-service grocery, wine, and beer stores. But even with her previous business experience, Ms. Snyder encountered some stumbling blocks during her early operations, particularly in marketing and finance.

Ms. Snyder did two things to overcome these hurdles. First, she was careful about the type of customer she sold her services to:

> I felt it was important to be selective in the beginning as to the type of customer I served because my reputation was very important. I was basically looking for entrepreneurs who needed my services while they established their businesses.

A second factor important to the success of MAILBOX was Ms. Snyder's willingness to take out a bank loan to establish credit.

> Every bank has a lending pattern. Find out what it is and take out a loan. It is critical that the small business owner establish a track record.

Ms. Snyder, who once had difficulty raising start-up capital because she lacked a credit rating, strongly emphasizes the importance of this step.

Also important to Ms. Snyder during early operations of MAILBOX was the support she received from her family. Her husband and four children were solidly behind her effort and eventually became involved in running the operation. Ms. Snyder found that this not only gave her confidence and the ability to persist until she had established her business, but that she was also rewarded by getting to know her children as adults and interacting with them in a new situation.

Business Skills

> *When I started my business, I realized that I knew a lot about my product, a lot about personnel management, and a lot about the industry. However, I felt very unsure of my skills in marketing and finance. Furthermore, I had no idea if the contracts I was signing with suppliers, a landlord, and potential customers were in my best interests legally. What did I do? I hired outside experts to advise me.*

From the beginning of your venture, you must understand your strengths and weaknesses in business skills. As was discussed earlier, most women entrepreneurs tend to be strongest in idea / product generation and in dealing with people, and weaker in finance and business planning. Recognizing that no one has excellent abilities in all business skill areas, you need to be prepared to compensate for deficiencies or weaknesses in areas that are important to your business.

Evaluating Your Own Skills

The first step is to determine the key areas of expertise needed in the business venture. For example, in a public relations or real estate business, marketing, sales, and people skills must be very good; in a manufacturing or construction business, operations and accountings skills are most important. You should determine the general areas in the business that must be problem-free and must operate consistently well to maintain a competitive edge. These key areas should be identified and prioritized.

The second step is to evaluate the level of your own business skills. Sometimes it is helpful to obtain opinions from a business colleague, a supporter, or a family member. Make sure, however, that these individuals know you want an honest, realistic appraisal, not ego building.

Third, you should match your strengths in business skills with the needs of the business. This will provide a clear idea of which areas need attention, both personally and for the business to ensure success. These needs will, of course, vary with the type and size of the business. How do you compensate for any deficiencies uncovered? There are several compensatory actions you can take, and many women entrepreneurs have relied on each of the following alternatives: hiring outside experts, taking on a partner, self-help through education, and appointing outside board members.

Florence Smith dealt with her weaknesses in a straightforward way. She started Kellner Equipment Company more than thirty-three years ago with only a typewriter, a telephone, and a thousand dollars in an industry where women were (and still are today) a novelty. Ms. Smith sold enough gas pumps, underground fiberglass fuel tanks, and nozzles to make Kellner the largest petroleum equipment supply house in the Pittsburgh area, with sales of over $2 million annually. Her biggest problems along the way were her fear of the banking community and developing the right organizational structure. How did she handle these problem areas?

I don't pretend to be what I am not: an engineer, a technician, or a financial expert. My forte is dealing with manufacturers and the customers on a personal level, so that's what I do. I have a reputation for being tough, yet nice on collections.

Ms. Smith relies on experts or professionals to complement her personal skills and has now put her people skills to use by becoming involved in civic and trade organizations. She has the distinction of being the first woman president of the Petroleum Equipment Institute, an international organization with more than 800 member companies in twenty-five countries.

Finding Outside Experts

Who are the experts and how do you find and evaluate them? There are seven major types of experts that you can hire to assist in your business: lawyers, accountants, insurance agencies, advertising agencies, manufacturers' representatives, management consultants, and market research firms. Most women entrepreneurs think that lawyers and accountants are the most important experts to consider.

The best sources of recommendations for these outside experts are personal contacts, your banker, business associates, or board members. It is important to evaluate any outside expert using the following procedure:

1. *Check References.* Find out what other businesses the expert has worked for and contact them. Ask if they were satisfied with the expert's work and whether they would rehire that individual.

2. *Interview the Expert.* Determine how the expert can help you and your business, based on previous experience, educational background, and problem-solving abilities.

3. *Compatibility.* Be sure the expert is someone you can work with and trust. While this is often a matter of intuition, your instincts are usually right.

4. *Interest.* Be sure the expert is interested in your business and will give you the advice and time you contract for. If you feel you are being "put off" when you have a problem, find someone else to do the job.

Linda Hutton, owner of a lacquer furniture manufacturing business, adds:

> It is difficult to determine how to hire experts. Women often need guidance on the types of questions to ask them. Generally, most lawyers and accountants will give an hour of free consultation and discussion before contracting for service. This is a good way to evaluate them.

Carol Bonner of Aircraft Technical Publishers in California suggests:

> Be sure that outside experts can be comfortably direct and honest with you. There is no point in paying people to tell you what they think you want to hear.

In addition to hiring an expert, another way to make up for deficiencies is through self-help methods such as continuing education, minicourses, or seminars sponsored by trade associations. There are many skill-building sessions offered through a variety of sources that can assist in teaching you the key elements of human relations management, personal selling, or any other specific subject that is required. The sources of information for continuing education were outlined in chapter 3.

On the subject of overcoming deficiencies, one woman entrepreneur commented:

> I realized that I was weak in business planning. After several consultations with an experienced business executive, I decided to invite him to serve on my board of directors.

By inviting experts to serve on the board of the new venture, you can ensure their commitment and interest in the business. Experts on the board will often be valuable in providing contacts, assisting with financing, and offering objective appraisals about the venture. Board members will often expect stock or some other type of equity interest in exchange for the services provided. When this is the case, you should consider the issue of control over the business when using board members as experts.

Finally, the option of taking on a partner is one exercised by many women entrepreneurs. In this case, as was discussed in the last chapter, it is vitally important that you and your partner be compatible and that the terms of the partnership be carefully delineated and documented.

Selecting Outside Firms

The Advertising Agency

In addition to lawyers and accountants, women entrepreneurs frequently find it necessary to hire an advertising agency and a marketing research firm in the early operations of the enterprise. In selecting an advertising agency, you should decide on the nature of the services your firm will need. A complete list of the services provided by an advertising agency is given in table 5–1. You should select carefully the services required, keeping in mind the constraints of your own time and the resources of the firm. Usually the most important service that an advertising agency can provide during the early operation stage of the new venture is copywriting.

Before actually selecting an advertising agency, you should prioritize the services needed and base your decision on the relative cost and money available. Once you have done this, you should consider several agencies that have had some experience in the industrial area of your new venture, and you can accomplish this initial

Table 5–1
Common Services Provided by
Advertising Agencies

1. Copywriting
2. Art techniques
3. Packaging design
4. Photography
5. Typography
6. Reproduction
7. Printing
8. Program planning
9. Public relations
10. Public speaking
11. Media analysis and selection
12. Market research
13. Space allocation
14. Trade shows
15. Sampling
16. Sales promotion
17. Others

Source: Robert D. Hisrich and Michael P. Peters, *Marketing Decisions for New and Mature Products* (Columbus, Ohio: Charles E. Merrill Publishing Co., 1984), 365–66.

screening by using information from friends or by telephoning several possible agencies.

You should then select two or three agencies from this initial screen that can be considered for final selection. Each of these agencies should be visited and evaluated using the checklist in figure 5–1. For each item on the checklist that is appropriate, you should assign a scale value from 1 to 5, with 1 representing the lowest rating and 5 the highest. The ratings total will at least give you a subjective quantitative basis for comparison of the various agencies.

Since cost is usually an important consideration in selecting an advertising agency, you should look for smaller agencies located outside the high-rent districts of the area. These smaller agencies often give better, more cost-effective attention to a new venture than do larger advertising agencies with sizable local or national accounts.

Item	Value
1. Location of agency	
2. Organizational structure of agency	
3. Public relations department services	
4. Research department and facilities	
5. Creativity of agency staff	
6. Education and professional qualifications of agency's top management	
7. Media department qualifications and experience	
8. Qualifications and experience of account executives (if identifiable)	
9. Interest and enthusiasm shown toward firm and new product	
10. Copywriter qualifications and experience	
11. Art director's qualifications and experience	
12. Recommendations by other clients	
13. Experience and success with new products	
14. Ability of agency to work with company advertisng department	
15. Extra services provided	
16. Accounting and billing procedures	
17. Overall formal presentation	

Source: Robert D. Hisrich and Michael P. Peters, *Marketing Decisions for New and Mature Products* (Columbus, Ohio: Charles E. Merrill Publishing Co., 1984), 367.

Figure 5–1. *Checklist for Advertising Agency Selection*

Also, you may find that some creative people in larger agencies will "moonlight" during their free time; they too can be a good, cost-effective source for advertising advice. In either case, you should assess carefully the creativity, interest, and compatibility of the individual who will be doing the work for the business before making the final selection.

The Marketing Research Firm

As was the case with an advertising agency, bigger is not always better when you are seeking a marketing research firm. In fact, since your goal is to obtain high quality research that has been efficiently and accurately designed and executed, smaller is often better.

What should you look for in evaluating and selecting a market research firm? Basically, you should evaluate each research firm in terms of five factors. First, the individual at the research firm who will be in charge of the project should be experienced and knowledgeable in research methodology and be accessible to you for discussion and consultation. Second, the person in the research firm (if not the one in charge) who is designing the questionnaire for the project should be familiar enough with the industry and the new venture to design an appropriate questionnaire. This individual must have the expertise and a sufficient amount of time to develop an effective questionnaire that will collect valid data. Third, the individuals doing the coding, tabulation, and analysis of the survey results must be well versed in all of the most accurate analytical data techniques and be able to generate a clear, tailor-made computer printout. The analysis and output should be relevant to the research project of the new venture and not just some preprogrammed, overused, general computer output. Fourth, the research firm should understand and be able to employ qualitative research methods such as observation and focus groups. The firm should have experience in these methods and know their limitations. Finally, the research firm should have experience in setting up and moderating focus groups (a focus group is a group of people brought together to discuss the particular problem). It is especially important that a good moderator be available who will be thoroughly involved in the project of your new venture from beginning to end.

So, using these criteria can help you to screen and select the marketing research firm that will be able to provide the most appropriate data for your new business at the best possible cost.

Test Marketing

Often it is important for you to get a sense of whether or not the market likes the various elements in the marketing plan. You can obtain this information from some form of test market. A test market provides a "laboratory" in which you can experiment and obtain the reactions of consumers on different aspects of the marketing mix, and simultaneously it provides data for determining that critical figure in the business plan—forecasted sales. Test marketing has a very broad scope and many interacting factors when it is done by large corporations, but you can modify many of the principles used in these large-scale operations for a smaller-scale application.

Considerations

You should consider three things in deciding whether or not to test market: time, costs, and production/technology constraints. As in all of your decisions at this point, time is probably crucial. Time will be taken up in designing, administering, and evaluating the results of the test market, and meanwhile a competitive enterprise can respond to the challenge of your new venture while you are awaiting the results of your test market. Second, test markets can be costly. While you need not engage in a full-scale national test market, as a Proctor and Gamble or Gillette would, even the low-budget market tests involve certain costs. You should carefully evaluate the importance of the information needed to help you make a better decision on some aspects of the marketing mix or the importance of the information needed to gain a loan from a financial institution before you accept the costs of test marketing. By looking at the test market in terms of information value, you can weigh the risks and costs of product failure against the probability and profit of success. Finally, in some situations a test market can be difficult to perform. Suppose, for example, that your new venture involves a new technology requiring the same investment regardless of the scope of the initial marketing effort. In this situation, a marketing effort in a smaller geographical area is usually preferable to a test market, because sales and market information are both obtained in this way.

Once you have decided to do the testing, you should select the appropriate test market. The choice of test market depends primarily on the nature of the product and its market segment. You should evaluate each possible location, using a modified version of the checklist in figure 5–2. Overall criteria for selection include general, product orientation, marketing mix, and control. The nature of the product and target market will make certain criteria more important than others. Once you have determined a geographic area, then the test experiment must be designed and sample size determined.

Alternative Methods

There are several alternatives to a true test market that involve much less time and cost. Although these alternatives will not provide the type of data a full scale market test would, they can still give you valuable information for modifying a market plan by reflecting reactions of the consumers. These alternatives include selling the product at a flea market, selling the product using a pushcart at an appropriate shopping area, selling the product through mail order, and selling the product at a home party. In addition to actually selling the product, you should try to obtain consumer opinions. If you only want opinions, you can obtain them by giving away free samples, talking to experts, inviting people to home parties to discuss the product, or by forming focus groups.

Focus group interviews have been used since the 1950s in many aspects of marketing research for products, legal trials, stores, and political candidates. This kind of interview is an excellent way for you to obtain consumer opinions on the product and on all aspects of the new venture. A focus group interview basically consists of a moderator and a group of individuals who engage in an open, indepth discussion. The group of ten to twelve people considers all aspects of the product and business in a discussion involving as little direction as possible from the moderator, but the moderator's presence ensures that the group sticks to the topic and provides information in the areas you consider important.

Through any of these informal test market alternatives, you can gain valuable information that you can use to determine the highest level of sales and the best marketing plan to achieve them. The results of these tests should of course be part of any business plan that you present to potential financial sources, for the test results not only support the figures in the plan, but show evidence of effort and capability on your part. For some women entrepreneurs, the results

| City or Region _____ |

| Criteria | Relative Advantage |

General	Good	Average	Poor	Does Not Apply
1. Representative as to population size				
2. Diversified in age, religion, and number and types of families				
3. Typicality in terms of sales potential for the tested product category				
4. Represents industry and employment				
5. Degree of isolation from other areas				

Product orientation	Good	Average	Poor	Does Not Apply
1. Stability of overall year-round sales				
2. Amount of product category sales				
3. Typicality in terms of sales potential for the tested product category				

Marketing mix	Good	Average	Poor	Does Not Apply
1. Typicality of wholesale outlets				
2. Typicality of number and type of retail outlets				
3. Representative as to advertising media				
4. Degree of cooperation of available advertising media				

Control	Good	Average	Poor	Does Not Apply
1. Degree of trade cooperation				
2. Degree of company control over entire test market operation				

Source: Robert D. Hisrich and Michael P. Peters, *Marketing Decisions for New and Mature Products* (Columbus, Ohio: Charles E. Merrill Publishing Co., 1984), 216.

Figure 5–2. *Checklist for Selection of a Test Market*

from a test market or alternative have been the deciding factor in securing needed capital.

The Need for Capital

Not only at start-up but throughout the entire life cycle of the business venture you will find one recurring theme—the need for capital at a reasonable rate. Since there are many different sources of capital for different needs, one of your most difficult tasks is knowing where to look. As one woman entrepreneur stated:

> While a woman may be very entrepreneurial, she usually does not know financing, the alternative types of financial arrangements, and where to look to meet her financial needs.

As this woman entrepreneur indicates, you need to know all the various sources of capital available. Many capital classification schemes exist, but perhaps the most useful is based on the type of input by the investor—active or passive.[1] Active investors want to have some inputs into the business's decisions as well as receiving financial returns; passive investors usually are only interested in financial returns.

Active Sources
Women entrepreneurs have found the following sources of capital useful.

The Entrepreneur. The source of funding employed most often by a woman entrepreneur is the entrepreneur herself. More than 99 percent of all new businesses obtain their start-up funds from personal assets and savings, and, limited as such sources may be, they are usually the only sources of capital available. Often, personal borrowing such as second mortgages on homes and other fixed assets are needed to generate sufficient funds.

Spouse. Spouses of women entrepreneurs can provide an additional source of funds. A spouse can frequently provide part of the initial capital for start-up, and the spouse's earnings can provide the personal and family support to allow the money needed for start-up to remain in the company.

Partner(s). When carefully selected, partners can not only provide needed capital, but business advice as well. However, a partnership arrangement rarely lasts for the duration of the new venture. For example, while more groups (partners) than individuals have started high-tech companies because of the risk involved, the majority of them have broken up because entrepreneurs want their independence. For a partnership arrangement to work, the background and skills of the partner must be complementary to those of the entrepreneur.

Informal Investor(s). When they can be found, informal investors will often provide one of the best sources of capital. Such an individual, often an entrepreneur who acquired capital from the sale of previous businesses, likes to take a very active role in overseeing the investment and making the business decisions. You should be careful, however, to see that the amount of active participation by the informal investor is in line with your own expectations and desires. An informal investor generally invests between ten and one hundred thousand dollars in a new enterprise, so a group of such investors is often needed to raise adequate capital.

Private Placement. Although used less frequently than other sources of capital because of the time and effort involved, private placement can provide you with needed funds. A private placement is similar to a stock offering, except that it is exempt from some of the requirements (prospectus, registration, contents, and disclosure) of the Security and Exchange Commission. There are, however, specific guidelines with regard to the amount of money raised, the information provided, and the number and type of investors involved.[2] The most popular private placement of issues up to five hundred thousand dollars is Regulation D. It allows the stock offering to be sold without registration to an unlimited number of purchasers using a brokerage firm. Different rules apply, of course, for the issuance of other securities and amounts. But a private placement, when successful, requires significantly more time and money than other sources of capital, with often a 10 percent to 20 percent brokerage firm fee. To obtain a private placement, you must provide a significant amount of venture information to many individuals, the majority of whom may not invest.

Private Venture Capital Firm. Private venture capital firms are by far the most well-known source of capital, but they rarely provide the money for starting new businesses. This source of capital comes with a lot of strings attached. Venture capital firms will typically invest from $250,000 to over $3 million in a venture over a period of several years, expecting an equity position usually close to 50 percent, and a return of five times the initial investment in three years—a yield of 67 percent compounded annually. While an investment rarely pays off in three years, the rate is used more to attain the venture capitalist's ownership position in the company. For example, suppose you are starting a business in an industry in which businesses are selling at ten times their annual earnings. If projected third year earnings for the new enterprise is $1 million, the firm would then have a value of $10 million (ten earnings multiple times $1 million). Since the venture capitalists want their $1 million initial investment to be worth $5 million in the third year (the 67 percent yield compounded annually), they would expect 50 percent of the company's stock.

Moreover, venture capitalists place a great deal of emphasis on the person as well as on the idea. As one venture capitalist stated: "Most venture capitalists do not invest in people who do not have significant prior work experience in the field of the new enterprise." When dealing with a venture capital firm, you should be sure that the terms of the investment agreement are not too restrictive and that the firm can provide more than just money. The venture capitalist should have a broad network of contacts providing access to bankers, suppliers, and even potential customers. Furthermore, there should be some agreement about the role of the venture capital firm in the next round of financing if needed.

SBICs and MESBICs. Small Business Investment Companies (SBICs) are investment partnerships between the U.S. government and entrepreneurs. Established by the government to provide equity for small business firms, SBICs have restrictions on and directives regarding the use of their very limited resources. Minority Enterprises Small Business Investment Companies (MESBICs) provide the same help exclusively to minority businesses. Except for perhaps minority women entrepreneurs, they provide very little opportunity for obtaining capital.

Development Corporations. In an attempt to increase employment, state and local development corporations have been established in some areas. They usually provide limited opportunity as a source of capital for the woman entrepreneur, for they have many restrictions and a very limited amount of capital available.

Research and Development Funds. If you are developing a new technology or a new product, you may be able to obtain some invention development money from the research and development funds of major universities and corporations. While of course the invention must be in an area of interest to the company or university, research and development funds provide an excellent source of "seed capital" to develop the technology perhaps to the prototype stage.

Passive Sources
The types of investors discussed up this point generally take more of an active role in the decisions and operations of the enterprise. There are other sources of capital available that tend to be more passive in nature—the investors merely supply the needed equity. Passive sources include family, friends, banks, commercial finance companies, insurance companies, pension funds, and public offerings.

Family. Next to personal savings, families provide more capital for women entrepreneurs than any other source. Family members usually are not as demanding about the timing of the loan repayment, often accepting it whenever it is available. If you have neither a track record nor enough personal assets, your family may be the only source of funds.

Friends. Like the family, your friends can often provide the needed source of funds. You should be careful to see that the repayment terms are clearly understood and mutually agreed upon.

Banks. The specifics of obtaining a bank loan are discussed later in this chapter, but the wide range of banking and lending services will be outlined here. When you apply for a loan, the bank will evaluate carefully both you and your business plan, especially the financial statements, before granting a loan. Five different types of loans are available: character loans, installment loans, lines of credit, commercial loans, and term loans.

Character loans are short-term unsecured loans to individuals or companies to be used for general purposes. This kind of loan can often be the best, but it is usually unavailable if you have a limited track record in business and credit. Character loans are only given when the applicant has an extraordinarily high credit standing.

Installment loans are a frequent source of capital for women entrepreneurs. These loans are made for any business purpose and often vary in amount season by season, depending on the financial need. Of course you need collateral to secure the loan; repayment is on a monthly basis. An alternative for seasonal financing and for building inventories are commercial loans, loans with repayment terms of thirty to ninety days.

Lines of credit are perhaps the most important financing provided by banks for the woman entrepreneur already in business. A line of credit from a bank indicates that a bank is willing to lend you money up to a certain limit at any time. Perhaps just as important as the reliable source of money is the message of confidence in you and in your enterprise that the bank sends out to other business associates by extending this line of credit to you.

Term loans are loans for a specified period of time, usually from one to ten years. Since they usually have higher interest rates and are therefore more expensive, women entrepreneurs use them to bridge the gap when other short term financing is not available.

Commercial Finance Companies. When banks will not provide the capital, you can approach a commercial finance company. These companies lend money secured by some asset of the company, such as accounts receivable or inventory. In other words, you can give accounts receivable, for example, to the commercial finance company as collateral for the money lent. Upon collection of the accounts receivable, you will repay the loan. One form of accounts receivable financing is called *factoring,* and in this system you can actually sell the accounts receivable to the commercial finance company for collection. Under this arrangement, any uncollectable accounts will usually be at the expense of the finance company. So, instead of accounts receivable, inventory is more often used as the security for the loan from the commercial finance company.

Insurance Companies. Life insurance companies do have significant funds for investment, but they are mainly limited to debt financing for large companies, with the exception of long-term real estate mortgages.

Pension Funds. Probably the newest source of capital for the woman entrepreneur is pension funds. Still mainly conservative in their investment posture, these funds are becoming more and more active in the riskier financing of small businesses. If this trend continues, in time pension funds may become a good source for capital for small firms for their resources are very, very large.

Public Offering. The final source of capital open to the woman entrepreneur involves the sale of stock in the company. This can rarely be done without a company track record (except in the case of very rapidly changing high technology such as biotechnology), and gaining this source of capital requires compliance with the regulations of the Securities and Exchange Commission.

Bank Loans and How to Get Them

Let us now turn to a thorough discussion of bank loans. Few aspects of business present as great a problem for the woman entrepreneur as obtaining a bank loan. As was outlined in chapter 1, women entrepreneurs often lack a financial track record and skills in financial planning, accounting, and business operations. Limited experience in executive management, making financial decisions, and negotiating exacerbates the problem. If the product or service proposed by the woman entrepreneur is nonproprietary (that is, not covered by a patent or license), the lender's risk increases. Sometimes, a married women entrepreneur has to have her husband cosign a note before a bank will lend the money. By contrast, male entrepreneurs, even those lacking a track record, probably have a credit rating, a home mortgage, and an education in a business or technical field. Furthermore, men are more likely to have friends in the banking community who are helpful in getting to the right person. So, from the bank's perspective, the woman entrepreneur without a track record often presents a greater risk than the male entrepreneur without a track record.

Although discrimination is sometimes mentioned by women entrepreneurs as the reason for their loan denial, it is difficult to say that this is the case. Banks usually evaluate fairly each applicant based on the ability of the business to repay the loan. Your positive attitude, preparation, and organized presentation can influence this evaluation.

Joanne Jordan, owner of J. Jordan's hair stylists, offers the following advice for obtaining the needed bank loan:

> On banking, learn about loan applications. You don't have to tell the banker everything, and you should find out why the information required by the bank is important. Ask them what they need to know to make the decision to give you a loan, then give them only that information.

What is the bank looking for? This varies from bank to bank, but according to Lynn Walsh of the Sailor's Valentine:

> Basically, when I went to the bank, they were looking for three things: my commitment to the project, a marketing plan, and some evidence that I had done my homework with the numbers.

As each of these two comments indicates, your success in obtaining a loan depends largely on your understanding the components of the loan application and how that application is evaluated by the bank.

The Loan Application

While each bank may have a specific loan application format, the application provides the bank with the two fundamental pieces of information: your credit worthiness and the ability of the venture to make enough sales and profit to repay the loan. This information must be provided on the application so that the bank officer can easily understand how the money will be used to increase the sales and profitability of your new enterprise.

There are usually eight parts to any good loan application: executive summary, business description, owner/manager profiles, business projections, financial statements, purpose of loan, amount of loan, and repayment schedule.[3] The loan application is based on the business plan discussed in chapter 4 describing what the business is, its directions in the future, and how the money lent will allow the future objectives to be attained in a profitable manner.

The Executive Summary. Each loan application should begin with an executive summary—a one-page summary of the entire loan application. This is often a very difficult part of the loan application, as it requires you to consolidate the information on the lengthy application into one, or, at most, two pages. This summary gives the loan officer a brief overview of the application by providing: your name, company, and address; a brief description of the business; the amount and purpose of the loan; and the method and schedule for repayment. Even though the executive summary is the first item in the loan application, you will probably find it easier to complete last, after you have become familiar with the entire application.

The Business Description. The second part of the loan application is the business description. It should thoroughly describe the business in terms of its organizational structure, products, markets, customers, and competitors. The background and history of the business should be described in terms of number of years in operation, sales, market share, inventory turnover, and previous successful marketing techniques. Samples of company brochures, advertisements, and sales promotion literature should be included.

Owner/Manager Profiles. The third section—the profile of the woman entrepreneur and any managers—should be developed to assure the loan officer that the management has the necessary skills, determination, and energy to attain enough sales to pay back the loan. While the paragraph or two on each individual should discuss educational background, work experience and accomplishments, and skills, a detailed resumé of each should be included in an appendix at the end of the application. Since this is an important part of the application and one that is not as quantifiable as the rest of the application, you should not be conservative or overly modest in this presentation. You should remember the old adage: "If you don't toot your own horn, your horn never blows."

Business Projections. Following the profile is the business projections section. It includes the forecasts of sales and market share for the next three years. As chapter 4 mentioned on the subject of preparing the marketing plan, these projections need to be supported by industry data from trade journals or trade associations, and by any actual marketing research that you have done. The projected increase in sales should of course be tied closely to the use of the loan you are requesting.

Financial Statements. The fifth part of the loan application contains balance sheets and income statements projected over the next three years using the format developed in the financial plan section of chapter 4. Where appropriate, historical balance sheets and income statements for each year of operation should be included. You should take care to ensure that the projections and financial ratios in the projections are in line with industrial trends and norms obtainable from the library or from the trade association of the industry.[4] When there is little or no business track record, your personal financial statement will probably be required.

Purpose and Amount of Loan. The next two sections of the loan application discuss the purpose and amount of the loan. Again, where appropriate, the forms in chapter 4 may be useful, particularly in indicating the exact amount of the loan required by detailing the specific estimates for each aspect; the use of these funds should be accurately indicated. Loans for purchasing fixtures, equipment, land, or buildings, with the cost estimates supplied, are more favorably evaluated by loan officers than are loan requests to increase working capital.

Repayment Schedule. The final section of the loan application is the repayment schedule. No bank loan officer will make a loan to an applicant without first making very sure that the business will be able to repay the loan as a result of the increased sales achieved through the use of the money loaned. The firm's income stream as demonstrated in the balance sheet and income statements should provide evidence that the future interest and principal payments can easily be met. Of course the life of the assets purchased through the loan must exceed the life of the loan.

Approval of the Loan—What Do Banks Look For?
What causes a bank loan officer to grant a loan request to one woman entrepreneur and not to another? According to Deborah Davis, who is in charge of commercial lending at a major bank:

> Banks look for experience in the field, at least one-third of the investment in the business by the woman entrepreneur, confidence and knowledge of the product or service, and preparation of a complete, well-documented loan package.

This view is supported by loan officers of other banks. Generally, banks calculate many ratios in their evaluation process. A list of these ratios and their calculations appears in table 5–2. Particularly important to the bank are the ratios involving the owner's equity. Some banks go as far as to calculate new balance sheets and income statements based on the equity of the woman entrepreneur in the business and on comparative industrial averages.

According to one study, the major purpose of small business loan applications was equipment purchase (54 percent), followed by property acquisition (19 percent), and working capital (15 percent).[5] The usual reasons for a loan application's being denied were (in order): poor credit rating, lack of competence, poor cash flow, poor market for product, poor collateral, and low equity.[6] Since women entrepreneurs are often weak in finance and have difficulty in developing a financially sound loan application, Martha Miles, a bank vice president, advised:

> If you are weak in finance, seek the help of an accountant. Many accountants will even go to the bank with you and help to secure the loan. If you don't know where to find an accountant, call your banker; he will give you the names of several in the area.

Two bank loan officers offered the following advice concerning another problem of women entrepreneurs securing a bank loan—the lack of confidence:

> One suggestion for gaining confidence is to interview or apply to several banks. Choose some that you would not expect to get a loan from just to gain the experience.
>
> Remember, you have something to offer the bank. There is nothing that says you cannot interview the bank first to determine the rates, procedures, and format before actually making a loan application.

While each bank has its own requirements and loan application evaluation procedures, it is clear that you must make sure that the loan officer of the bank can see that you are confident and that you have the motivation and competence to make the business such a

Table 5–2
Critical Ratios in Bank Application Evaluation

Liquidity: the ability of the company to meet its short-term obligations

Current ratio

$$\frac{\text{current assets}}{\text{current liabilities}}$$

Quick ratio

$$\frac{\text{current assets} - \text{inventory}}{\text{current liabilities}}$$

Leverage Ratios: the extent to which the company is financed by debt

Debt to total assets

$$\frac{\text{total debt}}{\text{total assets}}$$

Times interest earned

$$\frac{\text{earnings before interest and taxes}}{\text{interest charges}}$$

Activity Ratios: how well the company is using its resources

Inventory turnover

$$\frac{\text{Cost of goods sold}}{\text{average inventory}}$$

or

$$\frac{\text{sales}}{\text{average inventory}}$$

Average collection period

$$\frac{\text{receivables}}{\text{sales per day}}$$

Fixed asset turnover

$$\frac{\text{sales}}{\text{net fixed assets}}$$

Total asset turnover

$$\frac{\text{sales}}{\text{total assets}}$$

Profitability Ratios: management's overall effectiveness

Profit margin

$$\frac{\text{net profit after taxes (PAT)}}{\text{sales}}$$

Return on investment (ROI)

$$\frac{\text{net profit after taxes}}{\text{total assets}}$$

Return on net worth

$$\frac{\text{net profit after taxes}}{\text{owner equity}}$$

Return on sales

$$\frac{\text{sales}}{\text{owner equity}}$$

---

success that the loan will easily be repaid and that all present and future business of the company will be conducted with that bank. In order to avoid any delay in the bank's processing the loan application, Ms. Davis offered this advice:

> Make sure that the loan application package is complete. The more complete the package, the faster the loan decision can be made. Be sure to have previous loans with account numbers, balances, and telephone numbers. Most loan applications are held up because some minute data is missing.

Financial Analysis

Constant financial management is important for any woman entrepreneur to succeed in business. One of the most important areas in financial management is making sure that no major negative deviations from the budget occur. A budget deviation analysis should be done on a monthly basis in terms of the income statement and cash flow, using an adapted version of the forms appearing in appendix III, tables I and J respectively. For both cash flow and income you should compare the actual versus the expected on a number and on a percentage basis for each item, such as sales, cost of goods sold, and gross profit. This comparison will indicate to you any significant deviations that have taken place the previous month.

In addition to the monthly deviation analysis, each of the monthly cash flow and income statements should be accumulated on an annual basis. This merely means that you add the current month actual and budget to the last month's respective figures for each item so that a year-to-date number and percent deviation can be calculated. This year-to-date analysis allows a deviation one month to be easily corrected in the ensuing months. Since a small business usually has limited resources to take care of any major, prolonged deviations from the budget, this analysis on a monthly basis is one key for survival in the early operation of the business.

Promoting the Enterprise

Another frustrating area for the woman entrepreneur during the early operations of the new enterprise is the need to promote the

Table 5-3
Characteristics and Costs of Various Advertising Media

Media	Example	Rate Comparison Index	Factors Affecting Rate	Rate Base
Magazine	Consumer General business Trade Form	CPP = Cost per page × 10000 / Circulation	Number of readers Number of colors in advertisement Position of advertisement Type of audience Size of advertisement Volume discounts Frequency discounts	Page Part of page
Transit	Buses Subway Taxicabs	Cost per thousand exposures on riders	Number Position Frequency discounts	
Outdoor	Posters Painted displays Signs		Length of time Cost of production Frequency of audience counts Volume discounts Frequency discounts	Size of advertisement

Medium	Types	Cost formula	Pricing factors	Units
Radio	AM FM	$\text{CPM} = \dfrac{\text{Cost per minute} \times 1000}{\text{Audience size}}$	Time of day Size of audience Length of advertisement Volume discounts	Program 5, 10, 15, 30, or 60 second spots
Television	Network Local Cable television	$\text{CPM} = \dfrac{\text{Cost per minute} \times 1000}{\text{Audience size}}$	Time of day Length of advertisement Size of audience Volume discounts Frequency discounts	Program 5, 10, 15, 30, or 60 second spots
Direct	Letters Catalogues Brochures Coupons Price lists	Cost per contact	Postage Production Handling Mailing list	
Newspaper	Daily (morning or evening) Sunday Weekly Supplement	$\text{Milliline rate} = \dfrac{\text{Cost per agate} \times 1{,}000{,}000}{\text{circulation}}$	Number of readers Number of colors in advertisement Position Guaranteed charges Size of advertisement Volume discounts Frequency discounts	Agate lines Column inch

company and its offering in the best possible way with very limited resources. Deciding which media will most effectively reach the target market within the available budget can be difficult, so you should select the media that will provide the best cost per exposure. Each of the media types—magazine, transit, outdoor, radio, television, direct, and newspaper—is presented in terms of an example, the method for calculating a rate comparison index, the factors affecting the rate, and the rate base in table 5–3. Smaller start-up enterprises in their early years tend to get much more mileage from magazine, newspaper, and direct advertising. Of these, direct advertising and its extension direct marketing are so effective and important for you as an entrepreneur that they will be the focus of the next section. Trade journals and newspapers also offer a cost-effective way for visually displaying the company and its offering. When you have a small advertising budget, print media provide the most impact, for a picture is still worth a thousand words.

Two particular areas often overlooked by women entrepreneurs are new product releases and trade shows. One of the most effective ways to introduce a new product and company is to obtain as much free advertising as possible through magazines, newspapers, and trade journals. How do you accomplish this? By issuing news releases on the product, the company, and its executives, with an address and telephone number for obtaining more information. Some rules that will help ensure that such releases will be used by the appropriate media are shown in table 5–4. Since many trade journals and consumer magazines have new product sections, you should identify the appropriate ones and write a news release in the same style that has appeared in the respective magazine or journal. News releases written clearly and in the style of the journal need minimal rewriting and are consistent with the content and reader's interest. You should record by journal any inquiries received from a particular release, since the journals eliciting the greatest response are good candidates for future advertisements.

Another important area of promotion often overlooked by women entrepreneurs is trade shows. Each particular product category has one or more shows at which companies display their latest products to the trade dealers and to interested consumers, and these trade shows give you contact with many dealers from different

Table 5–4

Rules for Issuing New Product News Releases

The news releases should be identified as such when mailed to the editor.

The release should begin with the name of product and its most important features.

Condense the written news release to about 100–500 words to increase probability of acceptance.

Include a photograph of product that is high-quality and on glossy paper (firm may pay nominal fee to defray cost of printing the photograph).

Issue separate releases for each model and size to maximize the exposure of the new product.

Maintain file of sources and requirements needed to obtain news releases successfully.

---

geographic areas. For example, the largest trade show for novelty items is the consumer electronics show held in Chicago in January each year, while the largest computer trade show is held in Las Vegas each November.

The five primary objects of trade shows are indicated in table 5–5. You should evaluate those trade shows that seem to be appropriate for your company's product and then attend those, keeping the budget constraints of the firm in mind, that will provide the best exposure for your company and its product.

Direct Marketing

One of the easiest ways to obtain initial sales is through direct marketing. This approach allows your company to offer the product or service by mail or telephone to a target market and to solicit a response and obtain information.

Table 5–5

Objectives of Trade Shows

Obtain orders
Increase prospect list
Pass out literature
Demonstrate products
Increase knowledge of competitor activities

The best-known direct-marketing technique is use of catalogues and flyers. Retail and manufacturing organizations have used these for years to generate sales for a wide variety of products. Starting in the late 1960s and continuing today, sales by mail and telephone solicitation have expanded rapidly due to good word-processing capabilities, which allow for easier reproduction of form letters and retention of mailing lists; increased use of credit cards; and more women in the work force.

For you as an entrepreneur, direct mail provides a means for targeting specific individuals and soliciting their response on a more personal basis. As such, solicitation is not in direct competition with news, stories, or other advertisements in the media. The key factors for success in any direct-marketing campaign are identifying the target customers, preparing the mailing piece, and monitoring the results.

By far the most important asset of an established direct-marketing business is the mailing list—a list of the best and most likely customers for a certain line of products. You must identify potential customers by name and address. An enterprise just starting in a small geographic area can identify names from friends, professional colleagues, and the yellow pages, but when you need to reach a larger market, you may have to buy a mailing list from a list broker. The cost of the list depends on its size and nature. Generally speaking, the more screening that takes place for an individual to be included in the list, the higher the cost. For example, a list of individuals who make over thirty thousand dollars a year, are married with two children, and are college-educated and living in Hopkinton, Massachusetts, is more expensive per name than a list of individuals qualified only by two criteria; earning thirty thousand dollars a year in a specific geographical area. You can find list brokers in major cities under that heading in the yellow pages.

Once the list has been developed, a mailing piece must be carefully prepared to elicit a positive response from the individuals on the list. The piece must be interesting and should project a positive image of the product and the firm. Regardless of the size, the total visual presentation must assure the individual that the products being offered provide good quality for the money by a firm that is willing to stand behind them. A money-back guarantee often reduces the anxiety and risk involved for an individual trying the product.

This guarantee is particularly important when high risks are involved in trying a new product and a new firm.

The final factor for you to consider in direct marketing is monitoring the sales results achieved for each product. When multiple products and pages are involved in a catalogue, the sales and profit of each item should be compared with every other item; this will allow appropriate space to be devoted to each product in future catalogues. Also, the average dollar value of a customer needs to be determined. By knowing the total profit a customer will bring, you can ascertain the correct amount of money that should be spent on promotion to attract new customers.

Taxes and Your Business

When I first expanded my business, a restaurant, to more than forty employees, it was difficult for me to keep track of personnel and day-to-day operations, let alone paperwork. I found out very quickly that I had to stay right on top of quarterly income and social security tax filings. The government does not remind you to file, and if you miss the date, the penalties they enforce are very stiff.

The end result from successfully promoting and direct marketing the new enterprise is achieving sales, profits, and finally the inevitable part of business—taxes. Although the tax rate depends on the legal form of the organization and on the state in which the business is located, the business and personal taxes of the woman entrepreneur are still closely intertwined. The more money you can save on business and personal taxes, the more money you can invest in the early operations of the enterprise, when there is always a need for more funds. In a sole proprietorship or partnership, the income tax rate is at the rate of the individual (that is, the personal tax rate of the woman entrepreneur and each of the individual partners if any). The business itself is nontaxable. When the organizational form is a regular corporation, the organization is a taxable entity and is taxed at a lower rate than the personal rate. Any income that you draw out of the business is of course taxed at the personal rate. The Subchapter S form of organization has a different tax structure. While all business losses of the corporation directly affect the stockholders and their individual personal tax rate, any gains and distributions later paid out to stockholders are taxed as dividends, not ordinary income. As was mentioned earlier, this is the feature that makes Subchapter S corporations attractive to potential investors in high personal income tax brackets who want a loss to write off for the first few years of the new business's operation.

There are also several requirements that the woman entrepreneur must meet regarding income taxes for employees, and these are discussed very briefly below. As is the case with most tax laws, each of these requirements may have restrictions or exemptions, varying from one state to another, that you must carefully investigate to see if they are applicable. You can obtain specific information from a local Internal Revenue Service (IRS) or Social Security Administration (SSA) office, and you should review it with an accountant to determine exactly which taxes your business must pay and when.

You must secure an employee identification number by requesting one on Form SS–4, which can be obtained from a local IRS or SSA office. This number will be used on all correspondence with these agencies.

Wages subject to Federal Employment Taxes include all pay a business gives an employee for services performed. This may be in cash or other forms, including salaries, vacation allowance, bonuses, and commissions. Fringe benefits, sick pay, tips, supplemental wage payments and vacation pay may also be subject to withholding tax restrictions, depending on circumstances. To know how much income tax to withhold from an employee's wages, you, as the employer, should have a W4 Form on file for each employee, effective from the first wage payment. The employee is responsible for completing the form and itemizing deductions, but you must keep the form on record.

For you to deposit taxes, the Deposit Coupon from Form 8109, Federal Tax Deposit Coupon Book, can be used. These are preprinted forms, and they should be mailed to the Federal Reserve Bank in the regional area of your business according to instructions.

Most employers subject to income tax withholding, social security taxes, or both must file Form 941 regarding Return of Withheld Tax and Social Security Taxes on a quarterly basis. There are four categories of exempt employers; however, most businesses must file this form quarterly or be subject to criminal and civil penalties. You should determine the application of this tax to your business and be sure that filings are made properly and on time.

Federal Unemployment Tax returns (FUTA) must also be filed by employers on Form 940. This tax is usually a percentage of wages paid during the year, and there are allowances for credits against the FUTA tax amounts paid into state unemployment funds. Again, you should determine how this ruling affects your enterprise.

All tax records must be maintained for at least four years to be available for IRS review. An itemization of all the information required can be obtained from the IRS.

As mentioned before, many restrictions and circumstances may apply to your business, depending on its size and nature. You should seek complete information from your local IRS office, using the information here only as a guide.

Support Systems and Networking

In your own business, you do it alone. There is a definite need to find support groups to share your problems with. It is very important to be a part of the business community to legitimize your business and to gain general support for your endeavor.

As is the case in every phase of the new enterprise, you need a strong support system and an advisory panel, but you need them especially during the early operations of the new venture. This has certainly been Ellen McCaffrey's experience. She started Emily Business Systems, Inc., a service business offering computer forms and supplies, a little over two years ago. The business is constantly expanding geographically and in size. Ms. McCaffrey believes that the most important factor in her ability to establish her business has been a strong support base.

In the beginning, she obtained information from friends, business associates, and clients. Many of these individuals were also self-employed, and she found their willingness to share advice most helpful. Ms. McCaffrey also had a mentor who was similarly employed and offered important guidance on setting up systems and on the nature of the market. She thinks that trade associations, women's professional groups, and close friends were also valuable in her support system.

Ten years ago the word *network* usually meant a television station or perhaps referred to highway or railroad systems. Today, the word has an entirely different meaning; as one writer says, "It is the process of developing and using your contacts for information, advice and moral support as you pursue your career."[7] In other words, networking is an informal means of getting together with other people for business reasons. For the woman entrepreneur, networking is one way to establish an informal support group that can provide advice, referrals, industry information, moral support, clients, and friends. A network can also help resolve the main problem that many women entrepreneurs have: loneliness. Women business owners often lack colleagues at their level of business, and networks can help you to meet people in a similar position.

How do you find a network? Although most networks are not formally organized in the sense that companies are, many networks do have offices and regular meetings. You can involve yourself in a network through one of the following:

Women's networks

Trade associations

Personal affiliations—hobbies, school alumni groups, civic involvement, social groups, business associates, mentors, or friends

Women's Networks
Women's networks have recently received much attention because of increased efforts by women to create the equivalent of the "old boys network." In the past, most women were not concerned with careers, business, or self-employment, and hence there was little need to establish and use business contacts. Today, things are different, and women in general have recognized the importance of informal relationships with other business associates in order to gain information,

referrals, and advice. For the woman entrepreneur, establishing contacts in a women's network can be very helpful because women tend to have similar problems and often can offer emotional support that men cannot. Many women entrepreneurs feel that they gain more empathy and understanding from a women's network than from one including men. However, it is important for you not to rely exclusively on a women-oriented network because this will separate you from the real world where men are involved, and will keep you from being integrated into the system. (A listing of women's networks and trade associations is included in appendix I).

Trade Associations

Trade associations and networks that include both men and women are important in helping women entrepreneurs to keep up with new developments in the industry, and to establish contacts with counterparts and clients from other regions of the country and the world. These contacts and networks should be carefully cultivated to keep your business competitive. But how does a woman entrepreneur "befriend" male colleagues to be accepted into a trade network? Women entrepreneurs have suggested the following:

> *Dining in Groups.* As long as there are more than two people involved and the environment is relaxed, comfortable discussions can take place.

> *Hobbies and Sports.* Recreational activities can be a means to befriend male colleagues. Participation in a sport, like racquetball, or simply interest in a spectator sport is a way to develop a friendship. Hobbies can also provide common grounds for discussion.

> *Avoid Emotional Issues and Family Problems.* These topics are inappropriate for discussion in an informal friendship.

Ms. Bonner of Aircraft Technical Publishers offers this advice:

> Avoid gossip. Gossiping is a certain way to alienate any male colleagues. Do not try to approach men as another man would or use feminine charms to influence them. Be honest and be yourself.

Personal Affiliations

One final source of network contacts is your own personal affiliations; hobbies, school alumni groups, civic involvements, social contacts, business associates, and mentors can all provide a way for you to get involved in a network. Consider all personal associations as potential contacts for referrals, advice, or information:

> When I was starting my first venture, I was told to network. I first found it difficult to find one and then had no idea how to get involved.

As this comment by Janice Burling of Honeysuckle Hill Guest Inn suggests, getting into a network of contacts is not always easy. Probably the best tip is to use people skills. Most women entrepreneurs tend to have strong skills in human relations and this networking is an excellent way to use them. The following steps are also suggested:[8]

1. Make an effort to meet new people.

2. When you meet someone, search for common ground in your conversation.

3. Make mental notes of the other person's expertise and connections, and the possibilities for any joint projects you could work on.

4. Convey a positive impression of your abilities.

5. Remember what you talked about and follow up. Networking talk differs from ordinary conversation in that the purpose is to make a mutually beneficial contact. You should keep criticism to a minimum, avoid gossip, leave domestic conversation at home, and maintain a businesslike approach.

In general, most women entrepreneurs think that a combination of business-related (trade) and emotionally supportive (women-oriented) networks is most helpful. Maintaining contacts in both areas can give you confidence and support; these groups can also provide you with valuable industry information and help you to establish needed contacts for the future.

Entering Male-Dominated Fields

Women have difficulty establishing credibility with male business owners mostly because women tend to lack confidence and belittle their own achievements.

This comment brings up some issues that you must consider if you choose to establish your business in a male-dominated field. Most women entrepreneurs who are involved in construction, aviation, financial services, manufacturing, or other fields where women are in a minority have at times felt left out, unique, or occasionally uncomfortable because there are few women business owners in these areas. Three issues are commonly raised: first, the stereotyped view that women should be secretaries rather than business owners; second, a tendency for women to lack confidence because they are in a minority; and finally, negative feedback and discrimination because of gender.

Dealing with Stereotyped Views

Women are often stereotyped into certain roles no matter what their occupation. But the woman entrepreneur in a male-dominated field may have to confront more deep-seated views that women do not belong on a construction site, overseeing an assembly line, or in venture capital because these areas have traditionally been controlled by men alone. As a result, a woman entrepreneur who ventures into one of these areas may well encounter resistance and will often have difficulty being accepted as "the boss" rather than as an assistant.

Here are a few suggestions on how you can deal with role stereotypes:

> Most important, keep everything on a business level. Make sure you do not allow the issue of stereotypes to become more important than the business you are discussing. If you are asked to take minutes for a meeting, agree but suggest it be done on a rotating basis. Above all, do not become emotional about it.
>
> Be competent and decisive. Let clients and business associates know you are working hard, providing a high-quality product or service, and making decisions for the business.
>
> Acknowledge your gender, but don't use it as an excuse for success or failure. In the business arena, women entrepreneurs are business persons first and women second. Gender is irrelevant to the job you do.
>
> Be assertive, but not overly aggressive. Make sure clients and business colleagues know you will not be taken advantage of. Your concern must clearly be for the success of the business rather than emotional issues.

Building Your Confidence

Lack of confidence is also a problem for women entrepreneurs in male-dominated fields. This feeling usually has social causes, like the sense of being in a minority, rather than any real lack of knowledge about the business or product. It can, however, create problems for the business because tentativeness may be interpreted or misunderstood as a lack of knowledge or an inability to provide the product or run the business. Here are a few suggestions for dealing with a lack of confidence in this situation:

> Be prepared in any meeting, sales transaction, negotiating session, or other business forum. Have information organized, anticipate questions, and prepare answers accordingly. This will help to give you confidence.

> Know the industry, the market, and the business's product or service well. This will assist in building your credibility with clients and associates.

> Acknowledge that you are doing a job equal to or better than that of any men in the industry. Boasting is inappropriate, but gracious acceptance of praise where it is due and not belittling the achievements of your business are in order.

Overcoming Negative Feedback and Discrimination

Unfortunately, some women entrepreneurs do encounter negative feedback and outright discrimination upon entry into a male-dominated field. The feedback or discrimination can be subtle or overt as can be seen in the following comment by a woman entrepreneur in the machine parts business:

> At first, the buyer just said that they had already made arrangements for purchase of the machine parts they required. I accepted this until I found out that they were in fact still looking for the parts. When I recontacted the company, they said, in so many words, that they preferred to buy from a male-owned company where they could be sure of high-quality products and a lasting reciprocal arrangement.

What's more, the form of the discrimination can vary from one situation to the next. It can be based on perceptions of ability or intellectual capacity; it can be gender based, where your sex is the only issue; or it can be social, simply leaving out women entrepreneurs. Overcoming discrimination is difficult, requiring persistence and patience, but it is not impossible. Here are some recommendations for dealing with this problem that women entrepreneurs have found helpful:

> Concentrate on doing a professional job and avoid being overly emotional. If you get angry, restrain yourself, because anger will keep you from the professional job to be done and will serve no purpose in helping the business.

> Always act like a lady and treat men like gentlemen. Ignore sexually biased comments or criticism, and learn to respond by making a business-related comment.

> Try to anticipate situations that could bring negative feedback or result in discrimination. Focus on how to maintain a business-level conversation, so that if necessary, you will be prepared to redirect the discussion.

> Finally, have confidence that you belong. Hard work, professional behavior, and high-quality products or services have made your business viable. Therefore, it is the others, not you, who must get over the gender issue.

Perhaps the best advice of all is offered in the following comment by a woman entrepreneur:

> Don't waste time worrying about sex discrimination and being overly sensitive to attitudes that women are somehow different; just remain goal-oriented and dedicated, and work for the success of your venture.

6
Up and Running

Don't expand too quickly; do one thing well before you move on to the next stage. In our case, we were selling only cotton rag rugs and were tempted to offer more variety in styles and fabrics early in the game. We decided to establish ourselves with the cotton rag rugs before expanding, and it paid off.

I had to learn how to negotiate. Instead of simply offering my opinion or expresing my feelings openly when discussing my loan application with the bank, I had to learn to listen, ask questions, and make my decisions after thinking matters over.

There are two particular problem areas that confront women entrepreneurs once their companies are up and running, or about one to two years old. These issues are expansion and learning negotiating skills. Other areas that you will likely be concerned with at this stage are continuing education, maintaining support systems, and time management and control.

Carol Bonner, president and founder of Aircraft Technical Publishers, an eleven-year-old California-based business that sells microfiche products worldwide, is representative of women entrepreneurs at this stage. Ms. Bonner has seen her business develop from a product-building phase, with fewer than ten employees, to the present stage, with a major systems overhaul, expansion of new products into new markets, and more than seventy employees.

Important to Ms. Bonner is her association with trade organizations and her maintenance of informal groups of acquaintances with whom she can discuss business issues and mutual problems.

I prefer informal groups to formal associations; some tend to be run a bit like a sorority. I would rather meet with people of my level on an informal basis. Social contacts and a return to business school have facilitated this.

Continuing education was very important both personally and professionally for Ms. Bonner. She attended Harvard Business School for a series of three-week sessions over three years to participate in the Owner/President Management Program. She studied subjects like strategic planning, finance, and marketing, which she believes were essential to her planning for the expansion of her business. In addition, she made many friends and valuable contacts among executives running businesses of similar size from all over the world.

What advice does Ms. Bonner have for women who are just starting out in their endeavors?

The most important asset you can have is belief in the value of the product. If you believe in your product, then you will always have the strength of that conviction to pull you through those inevitable rough times.

The Importance of Continuing Education

My business had been operating two years when I realized how much I didn't know about marketing my products. A colleague of mine suggested a weekend workshop on marketing at the local college, which I attended. I am amazed at how much it helped.

As these women's cases suggest, continuing education at this stage of business development can be a good idea. Although education often implies "school," formal classroom instruction is not the only avenue by which to update skills or learn new management techniques. As was discussed in chapter 3, there are many potential sources you can consider for further education in preparing to start your venture. But, at the up-and-running stage time constraints will be different because you are now managing the business instead of just preparing for it. Therefore, the types of educational resources more appropriate for this stage are different. They include the following:

Workshops or seminars sponsored by Small Business Development Centers, the Service Corps of Retired Executives (SCORE), the Small Business Administration (SBA), or trade associations. These are especially appropriate when you are operating a business because the seminars and workshops are usually shorter, more concentrated, more information-specific, and less expensive than a full-credit college course. You should choose seminars or workshops on the basis of their applicability to your business, rather than just on your interest in the area.

Adult education courses or night courses are another way to improve skills at this stage, because these kinds of courses tend to be widely offered, meet in the evening, and are not that expensive. Again, your criteria for selection should be applicability to the business and skills needed.

Trade conferences and meetings with experts are a third method many women entrepreneurs have used to continue learning after they have established their venture. Trade conferences can give you pertinent industry information in a short period of time. They also usually sponsor smaller special sessions that allow for discussions of issues particularly relevant to a problem, business skill, or industry trend. Meetings with experts are also an effective way to gain information on specific problems or issues quickly.

Reading periodicals (both trade and general business) is another excellent way for you to continue learning. Several periodicals, both industry-specific and general, should be part of your regular reading. For example, a woman owning an advertising agency may want to include *Advertising Age* and *Sales & Marketing Management Magazine* (both industry-specific), as well as the *Wall Street Journal, Fortune* magazine, and a local newspaper (all general), on her reading list. (See appendix II for a listing of general periodicals.)

Finally, you should encourage any employees of the business to continue their education. If possible, consider company payment for conferences, workshops, or adult education classes because this not only builds the skills of the employee, but loyalty to the business as well.

Support Systems—You Still Need Them

*In the beginning, I made numerous contacts and attended as many
meetings as possible to establish contacts and learn what I could.
Now that I've settled into my business, I am more selective about
the contacts I maintain.*

This quote articulates the feeling that many women entrepreneurs
have at this stage in business development: their major concern at
this time is working hard to keep the business going. They have
achieved some measure of success by establishing their businesses
and therefore have more confidence, so they tend not to require the
same kind of business and emotional support mentioned in earlier
chapters. The advice to you at this up-and-running stage is three-
fold: you should maintain the basic moral, business, and network
support systems you have established, evaluate the types of support
given and match them with your needs, and finally, be selective and
modify support systems as necessary.

Moral Support System
The importance of a three-level support system—moral, business,
and networks—and its benefits have been emphasized in earlier
chapters. You should continue to maintain a moral and emotional
support base of family, friends, spouse, and mentor. While not to
the same degree as at start-up, some women entrepreneurs feel they
still need encouragement, even though their business is now operating. The reason? Once she has proved that she can run a business and
manage family responsibilities, she may find that people in her support system begin to take for granted all that she is achieving. Because
the woman entrepreneur has learned to accomplish many things in
her dual roles, people sometimes forget that the responsibility requires a great deal of stamina, organization, and optimism.

One woman entrepreneur related that she had once had to leave
her business during peak hours to deliver diapers to her home so the
babysitter would not have to take her toddler, who had a head cold,
outside in thirty-degree weather. This kind of interruption and fragmentation of time is often difficult. Just because you have learned to
quickly resolve family crises while running a business doesn't mean
that you need any less emotional encouragement. Hence, you should

make your needs known to your personal supporters, and if they are not understanding and encouraging, you should find someone who is.

Business Support System

You may also need to evaluate the business support system at this time in terms of the type of advice you are receiving. The experience of running the business has given you a good base of knowledge, as well as a clear idea of what guidance you need. You should assess all those involved in the business support system, from buyers to suppliers to clients, for their support, follow-through, and contributions. You may find it necessary to find new business supporters, or to be selective about those with whom you maintain regular contact. Each individual's interest, knowledge, and compatibility are criteria to consider.

Networks and Trade Associations

Networks and trade associations are the final support system you should evaluate. Like Ms. Bonner, some women may opt for informal rather than formal networking at this point. Now that you have had experience in the business and exposure to different organizations, you can better judge the merits of formal versus informal associations. Either way, follow-up and maintenance of contacts is important.

The up-and-running stage is also the point at which many women entrepreneurs feel more comfortable integrating themselves into either formal or informal male-dominated networks. Because a woman entrepreneur has established her business, she has achieved a level of credibility and will thus have less difficulty being accepted by these groups than she would have at earlier stages.

Negotiation in Eight Steps

We had the problem of wanting to get into a major distribution network without being taken advantage of. Each distributor wanted one rug in each color with no maximum or minimum order. It was difficult to determine where to draw the line.

A woman entrepreneur should develop her negotiating skills as quickly as possible. Women tend to be weaker in negotiating skills than men. This may reflect the level of issues typically negotiated at home versus in a business situation. These skills can be learned and then must be practiced.

In any business, an important part of success is the ability to negotiate. The term can be difficult to define, perhaps because we are so accustomed to negotiating that we do not realize we are doing it. Negotiation is the process by which parties attempt to resolve a conflict by agreement. Although it is not always possible to resolve the conflict by negotiation, the negotiation process can at least identify the critical issues in the disagreement. Negotiation is a process central to business dealings and is a skill that can be acquired. In fact, you negotiate every day at home with your spouse, or children, or with repairmen. So, while negotiation is not entirely new, the form of it and the environment in which it takes place are both similar and different. While there are many ways for you to develop negotiation skills, perhaps the most effective and easiest is to adopt an eight-step approach. These eight steps are: prepare, discuss, signal, propose, respond, bargain, close, and agree.[1]

Prepare

Preparation is probably the most important step in the negotiation process. Before the negotiation actually starts, you should define carefully what has to be done and develop some alternatives for accomplishing these goals. This process involves establishing the objectives that you want to achieve and prioritizing them according to which ones must be achieved, which should be achieved, and which you would like to achieve. Careful determination of each of these three types of objectives is essential before the negotiations actually take place. These objectives should take into account the position of your opponent, as well as your own knowledge. You can use this information about the opponent to support your position during the negotiation process.

Discuss

The next step in the negotiation process is to discuss. While arguing for a point may be an inexperienced negotiator's first instinct when confronting an individual with a different opinion, this should be avoided at all costs. Some of the dos and don'ts of discussion are indicated in table 6–1. By far the most critical "do" is to listen. The art of listening well is a rare one. You should develop the habit of listening carefully to what is being said and determining on which points the opposition shows some flexibility and which points are top priority.

Of the "don'ts" listed in table 6–1, the one most difficult for an inexperienced negotiator to avoid is talking too much. A good negotiator says as little as possible, especially before she has assessed the situation, and instead listens carefully. Be careful not to compensate for any nervousness by talking too much. It is not only unprofessional, but it also often results in your making too many concessions.

Signal

The third step in the negotiation process is signaling—the process that moves the negotiation forward to a solution. Signaling is a method of testing the opposition's willingness to change positions and then determining whether the objections raised are real or false. You need to learn how to discern whether objections raised are based on power, lack of confidence in the negotiations, or lack of information. A signal is of course a message to the opposition that you are willing to qualify the position presented. For example, your opponent is giving a signal that a solution is possible when a statement like "I can never agree to that" becomes "I can never agree to that in its present form." You must learn not only when and how to signal yourself,

Table 6–1
Dos and Don'ts of Discussion

Dos	Don'ts
Listen	Attack
Question for clarification	Blame
Summarize issues	Interrupt
Challenge on an item-by-item basis	Make threats
Be noncommittal about proposals of opponent	Point score
Determine priorities of opponent	Shout
	Talk too much
	Argue

Source: Adapted from Gavin Kennedy, John Benson, and John McMillan, *Managing Negotiations* (London: Business Books Ltd., 1980), 48.

but also how to read a signal from the opposition, and reading signals, of course, requires good listening.

Propose
Once you have read a signal, it is time for you to venture and discuss a proposition. The most important part of a good proposition is the point of departure from which further movement will probably occur. It can be very difficult for you to know at what point to open; this decision is highly subjective, depending on the content of the negotiations and on the opposing side. Although you really only learn this art after being involved in several negotiations, the main idea that you should remember is always to open at a realistic point and move slowly to the next point. All conditions of the proposition should of course be spelled out.

Respond
The sixth step in the negotiation process is the response to the proposal. A response should take into account the interests and limitations of the other party, but does not necessarily have to contain any concessions. If concessions are offered, they should be carefully and thoughtfully considered, taking into account the cost to you and the value to the opposition. Again, any concessions should reflect an assessment of the priorities of the opposition.

Bargain
Another difficult step in the negotiation process is bargaining—the process whereby something is given up for something gained. In bargaining, you should keep in mind the rule that nothing is given away free. The best way to ensure that you do not give anything away is to make everything you offer conditional—that is, give something only on an "if . . . then" basis. An "if" preceding the concession indicates that it will be given only if something else is offered in return.

Close
As every good salesperson knows, closing the negotiation is also an art. Closing is most easily accomplished by using either of two techniques: closing based on a concession or closing with a summary. As

the term implies, when you close with a concession, you are offering a concession to secure an agreement. This means conceding on a major element in the demands of the opposition, something like the following: "All right, I will reduce the price by one dollar per unit if you agree to sign the sales agreement now for five thousand units to be delivered next month." A summary close is used when many issues have been discussed; it simply means in this situation summarizing everything that has previously been agreed upon.

Agree

Of course the final step in the negotiation process is reaching a mutually satisfactory agreement. While you should not expect every negotiation to end in an agreement, it is the obvious objective of every negotiation. When an agreement has been reached, the details should be written down before anyone leaves. The most important rule of agreement is that it should always be recorded as specifically as possible before anyone leaves the negotiation area.

The End Result

These then are the eight steps that you can use in each negotiation process. The end result of the negotiation depends of course on the relative power and flexibility of the individuals involved. Although it is not easy to learn to negotiate and few people are really good negotiators, if you can acquire the skills, you will have an advantage in successfully running your business. Perhaps one of the most difficult negotiation areas will appear when you are planning to expand your business.

Expanding the Business

My business has reached the point where expansion is necessary. We either have to add on to our facility or open another store. I'm not sure which is best, and I'm a little apprehensive about making any snap decisions.

You should be careful not to expand the business too quickly, but a successful business is bound to grow. This growth can take place internally and externally—internally through expansion into new markets or new products, or externally by acquiring new businesses.

Internal Expansion

Internal expansion depends on the nature of your business and can be generally thought of in terms of expansion of products, markets, or both, as indicated in figure 6–1. The matrix in figure 6–1 offers four alternatives for consideration. First, market penetration means attempting to gain more sales to present customers with present products by making changes in the marketing mix (that is, by increased advertising, obtaining better shelf space, promotional pricing). Second, market development involves increasing sales by offering the same product to new markets, either geographic, demographic, or by type (consumer, industrial, institutional, or international). Product development or modification involves changing the actual product or creating a new one, but maintaining the same market; for instance, the color, style, size, or ingredients might be improved. Finally, sending new products to new markets is the last and most risky option, because the newer the situation is to the enterprise, the greater the risk and therefore the greater the potential return.

Generally speaking, the best principle for you to follow is to work from the strengths of your business. If the business has a strong research and development area and has been successful on previous occasions in introducing new products, then it should continue introducing modified or new products. If research and development is not a strength, however, then you should consider expanding into new markets with existing products. These new markets

	Products	
	Same	New
Same	Market Penetration	Product Development
New	Market Development	Diversification

Markets

Figure 6–1. *Growth Opportunity Matrix*

should be as similar as possible to ones in which the business is already successfully competing in order to decrease risk.

The issue of internal expansion can be a problem because the way the business must be managed changes. This change is often exemplified in the difference between being the boss and being the manager. Joanne Jordan had more than fifteen years of experience managing beauty salons, as an operator, manager, and owner of her own business. She believes that the key in her business is experience and communication; being available to listen to workers and customers is essential. Ms. Jordan emphasizes this point in this comment:

> I had fifteen years of experience in the field, and when I was asked to be the boss, I learned that being in charge does not mean you are a good manager. I ordered people to do things and this was not well received. In my second managerial experience, I went the other way and tried to be everyone's friend; then I found it tough to fire them. Finally, I feel I have reached a happy medium.

Today, Ms. Jordan's hair salon employs three stylists, and she plans to expand to six in order to offer more new services. Though her business has only been established for a little over a year, she has had many inquiries for employment and has outstanding rapport with her workers and clients.

External Expansion—Acquisition

Another way to expand the business is externally through acquisition. The acquisition of another business provides additional resources and a new direction for your business. The additional resources may be in the form of new markets, new productions, new distribution systems, new sales force, new products, new technology, new management, or new financial resources. The new aspect(s) of the business being acquired should complement the direction and efforts of the venture you already have. But how should you evaluate this potential new business? And perhaps more important, how will you finance the acquisition?

Evaluating a business for acquisition is indeed a difficult task, as can be seen in the problems encountered by acquiring corporations of all sizes. Often these problems result from total reliance on financial analysis. This method of evaluation focuses on profit and loss

figures, balance sheet ratios, and operating statements for the past
five to ten years that the firm has been in business. Financial analysis is important in the evaluation process, since a well-managed
company will be financially healthy, but it does not give a complete picture, particularly of a small company in a quickly changing industry. For example, a small company with an umimpressive
financial track record may be on the verge of a technological
breakthrough or may have a strong position in a market niche. In
evaluating a potential business for acquisition, you should look at
the firm's product lines and market position; its research and
development, marketing, and manufacturing capabilities; and its
overall management capabilities, in addition to evaluating the financial health of the enterprise.

Product Lines and Market Position. The first area—product lines
and market position—should be evaluated in terms of historical,
present, and future perspectives. The strengths and weaknesses of
the product line that have brought the firm to its present position
should be examined in terms of technology, patents, design, quality, reliability, and prices. You should evaluate the present share of
the market that the firm holds, as well as the diversity and size of the
customer base in order to ensure a reasonable market position with
no concentration on very few customers. Moreover, you should see
to it that the products of the business are compatible with those of
your own business from a marketing, manufacturing, and production point of view. If there is a poor match in these areas, integration will be time-consuming and costly. The future of the market
niche is perhaps the most important aspect; the business under consideration should be in a market that is growing and free from vul-
nerability to severe business downturns and competitive pressures.
In addition to relying on outside sources of information, you can
use the internal information of the business. If there is little information available within the firm or if that information is inaccurate,
perhaps you should not acquire the business.

Research and Development, Marketing, and Manufacturing. The
second area—the firm's capabilities in marketing, manufacturing, and
research and development—is one of the most difficult to evaluate.

The research and development aspect should be evaluated in terms of the dollar amount spent, whether the research is integrated into the firm's long-range business plan, and whether the output was worth the costs involved. Furthermore, the research and development should result in the successful introduction into the market of the innovations conceived. One good gauge of a firm's capabilities is the number of new products conceived each year and the number successfully introduced into the market place.

Closely allied with research and development and product innovation are the marketing and manufacturing skills of the business. You should determine the nature and quality of the marketing and manufacturing capability. What is the strength of the company's sales force or distributors? What channels of distribution are used? How do customers and noncustomers perceive the company and its products? What is the amount of money spent on promotion? What are the facilities and skills in the manufacturing process? How flexible and up-to-date are they? What is the quality of the output? The answers to these and other questions will provide you with enough information to make sure the manufacturing, marketing, and research and development areas are as strong as need be and are compatible with your business.

Overall Management Capabilities. The overall management capabilities of the firm being acquired should also be examined. The intensity of this evaluation of course depends on the type of integration that will take place when the acquisition is finalized. You will have to make a more critical examination if the management will basically be left intact or if you are searching for a successor to manage the entire operation. Regardless of the level of integration, you should determine which management personnel are responsible for each year's profit and loss results. In addition, you should assess the quality and characteristics of management in terms of their ability to cope with the challenge of the future.

Financial Health. Finally, you should perform the standard financial analysis of the business—earnings ratios, debt ratios, inventory turnover, cash flow, and capital structure—using the same techniques that banks use in determining whether or not to grant a loan (these ratios are discussed fully in chapter 5). Other issues to be addressed include how much the firm is actually worth and what the financial analysis indicates when you consider the firm's prospects for growth in sales volume and profits.

Financing the Acquisition. As you decide whether or not the business being acquired matches your business and objectives, you need to answer the question of how the acquisition will be financed. Besides the usual sources of funds discussed in chapter 5, a frequently used method for acquisition is the leveraged buyout. A leveraged buyout allows you to invest little if any of your own money to acquire the assets or stock of the other business. Instead, you can use the assets of the company being acquired as collateral for loans on the down payment and capital needed in the initial operations of the business. Leveraged buyouts are a possibility when the assets of the business being acquired are carried on the books at preinflation prices and the value of the business is depressed. In this situation, the assets provide ample collateral for an asset-based loan, which is the essence of a leveraged buyout. While leveraged buyouts have been successfully used by some women entrepreneurs, you should be careful to ensure that the potential sales and profits of the firm being acquired will provide enough cash to pay back the loans and other debts incurred. Leveraged buyouts are particularly risky when the management of the firm being acquired will not stay on for at least the first few years following the acquisition.

Time Management and Control

I often feel like a Raggedy Ann by day's end; I suppose it's because there are always a million more things to do after I've done the first million.

The up-and-running stage is where time management becomes a problem for many women entrepreneurs. Because most women business owners have had limited management experience prior to establishing their venture, becoming an effective manager and learning to manage time efficiently can often require some adjustments. Why is time management important? Mainly because time is a resource that cannot be bought or recaptured. To use time wisely requires analysis and planning.

First, determine where your time is presently being spent. Time is often difficult to track down. Most women entrepreneurs only know that they spend a lot of time working in their businesses, but few have any idea of the proportion spent in planning, at meetings, supervising, decision making, or resolving client problems. Maintaining a log for a week is one way to determine where your time has been spent.

Once you have an idea of your present time allocations, you can figure out how you would like to be spending your time. This is the planning part of time management.[2] You should establish goals and objectives based on the amount of time you want to spend in certain activities. Be realistic in these calculations because telephone interruptions, employee conflicts, drop-in sales people, and meetings will inevitably interfere with your daily plans and affect your goals. The prudent time manager will also try to avoid wasting time through personal disorganization, lack of priority setting, indecision, and accomplishing tasks that could be delegated to someone else.

Here are some suggestions that may prove helpful in managing time:

Analyze your use of time, otherwise your time will be spent where it should not be.

Anticipate events and plan accordingly.

Allocate time based on realistic estimates.

Set priorities and impose deadlines for accomplishing tasks.

Zero in on problems rather than on symptoms.

Avoid procrastinating, or postponing of decisions.

Be decisive.

Consolidate, streamline, and eliminate repetitive tasks.

Communicate clearly and concisely.

Delegate operational tasks and maintain planning responsibilities.

Take time for "human relations," but avoid oversocializing.[3]

In all, these suggestions may seem to be common sense, but most women entrepreneurs can benefit from the self-discipline in managing time that following these suggestions requires.

7

Managing the Enterprise

As much as I didn't want to admit it, my business has evolved through all the classic stages of business growth over the past eleven years. The characteristics and problems associated with each stage from development to expansion were clearly applicable to my business.

S haron Donegan of Boyle/Kirkman Associates indicates that her business, like most, went through several stages of development. For every woman entrepreneur, each stage is different and requires dealing with different issues and responding to various changes. The period immediately following the establishment of the business was discussed in chapter 5. Chapter 6 covered the up-and-running stage. Given that most women-owned businesses are young, it is also appropriate to consider the characteristics and issues that develop during the period following the establishment of the business. We divide this period of the enterprise into three stages: the stage in which a business is two to four years old and has established a track record; that in which a business is five to ten years old and is an established organization; and finally, that in which a business is ten years old or more and has become a mature company.

Track Record Established

One characteristic of the two- to four-year-old enterprise is that sales are consistently being made and the operation is growing. The business has some credibility in terms of its ability to produce the product or service in the eyes of its customers and competitors. As one woman entrepreneur remarked about this transitional stage:

> Two years had passed when I finally paused to assess the business. I was surprised that the business had survived so long in its initial form and realized it was time to make some changes.

Women entrepreneurs indicated that their concerns at this stage tend to revolve around management and personnel problems and obtaining new sources of capital. Some women business owners experience time conflicts between work and personal life. The woman entrepreneur is usually still the central authority in the business at this stage and continues to make nearly all the decisions under uncertainty.

There are several prescriptive steps a woman entrepreneur should consider at this stage. They include organizational changes, establishment of management control systems and record keeping, identification of new sources of capital, marketing mix changes, and maintenance of support systems.

Making Organizational Changes

Organizational changes should be reflected in modifications to the organizational chart outlined in chapter 4. All employees should have clearly written, updated job descriptions, and lines of authority should be clearly delineated. This will ensure that there is little overlap in effort and no conflicts between individuals. It is often at this stage of growth that you will find it necessary to write a company handbook setting forth policies in all management and personnel areas. This handbook might cover such areas as:

Organizational chart with reporting responsibilities

Job descriptions of all employees

Personnel policies with regard to hiring, promotion, termination, grievances, terms of employment, sick leave, and vacations

Insurance benefits

Profit-sharing plans

General operating procedures

It is important to comply with federal and state laws regarding labor, occupational safety, equal opportunity, and social security. Any applicable laws should be included in the handbook, along with the company's policy on the subject.

You may find it appropriate to consider delegating some authority for day-to-day operations to an assistant in order to devote more time to planning and building the operation. Although surrendering control is often a difficult step for a business owner, there comes a time when one person cannot do it all. In fact, consultants say that good executives will let subordinates make day-to-day decisions and save the weightier problems for themselves. Also, the stress of the disparate roles of business owner, wife, and mother often reaches a peak at this stage. Delegating operational supervision can give you more flexibility and free time.

One organizational means of dealing with this pressure involves team building or horizontal management. Many women entrepreneurs feel more comfortable with a horizontal style of management, in which the decision-making style is participative rather than directive. Depending on the size of the business, this type of management can involve establishing teams with rotating team leaders. Each team is responsible for its own area, with latitude in establishing how its product/service goals will be met. Each team should have clear communication lines with management, and management should in turn, evaluate and monitor the teams frequently. Teams are also good at problem solving and new product brainstorming, and with proper incentives, enthusiasm can be kept very high.

Establishing Management Control Systems and Keeping Records

Next, establishing management control systems and maintaining records are essential for a two- to four-year-old business. Once you have guided your business to a viable level, you should develop some means for assessing how it arrived there and where it should go. Typical areas to be considered are:

Paperwork Flows. Requisitions, receivables, payables, and general company communications should move efficiently within the organization and be taken care of as promptly as possible.

Sales Records. Complete records of buyers should be on file, with information regarding amount purchased, dates, contact person, and reorder information. A composite list of all customers and sales statistics should be made on a yearly basis to determine whether or not the company is attracting repeat customers, what the geographic sales areas of the business are, and all relevant trends.

Customer Service. Procedures for dealing with customers should be reevaluated and updated or modified, depending on the growth of the business. Soliciting customer feedback on the level of satisfaction in this important area is one method of evaluating effectiveness.

Employee Training. Any changes in internal systems developed from new laws, industry trends, or experience may require employee training. Since consistency of delivery and service is always the goal, making sure that employees are well trained is one way to attain that goal.

Efficiency. Investigate more efficient means of doing business. Time-saving devices, shortcuts on the job, computer assistance, a modified telephone system, or reorganization of work loads may be helpful in achieving greater efficiency.

Identifying New Sources of Capital
Third, it may be time for the two- to four-year-old business to seek new sources of capital to support the growth and expansion. You may have encountered difficulties in funding your business at start-up, but now that you have established a track record of operation, institutional sources and others are likely to be more willing to provide any needed funds.

At this stage you need to decide the size of the needed funds and whether or not you want to give up some of the ownership of the business. The latter question may have only one answer if the needed funds are large and the capital structure of the firm small. The size of the infusion of capital at this stage should be large enough (if possible) to sustain the firm for the next two to three years so that new capital sources will not have to be tapped for a period of time. Try to avoid constantly soliciting financing as it may appear that your plans for the financial requirements of the firm have been inadequate. Various types of bank loans are available to your firm at this stage in its development: lines of credit, collateral loans, inventory loans, factoring accounts receivable, and lease financing. The length of time of repayment, the amount, and interest rates depend on the specific conditions of the firm, and you should approach several banks in order to obtain the best terms possible. An ongoing business with a successful track record is a good investment for a bank, particularly now that the banking environment in the United States is so competitive.

If no other source of equity capital is present and the amount of money needed is large, this may be the time for you to seek venture capital. The venture capital market is a dynamic one consisting of participating investors who want involvement in an enterprise for about five to ten years. A formal business plan (as outlined in chapter 4) should be prepared and effectively presented. In determining whether or not to infuse funds into the enterprise, venture capitalists will be concerned with the product, the market, the financial statements, the track record of the business, and your experience. Try to make sure that the relationship with the venture capitalists will not be a stormy one before entering into any agreement that will affect the business for at least the next five to ten years.

Marketing Mix Changes
Fourth, the growth that your business has undergone may require major changes in the marketing mix. The product itself may need to be improved, changed, repackaged or modified to compete better. If the business is a service, it may mean extending the hours of operation, offering more personal service or new "wrinkles."

If the competition is particularly stiff, the price of the product or service may need to be reevaluated. A change in price can be very risky, however, as the competition will usually respond accordingly. Unless the business has the resources to withstand substantial cuts, a price decrease offers little long-run competitive advantage. It may be more reasonable for you to consider promotional pricing (temporary cuts, like two items for the price of one), quantity discount pricing, or other possible means to stimulate sales.

You may also need to review your channels of distribution. If the product or service is reaching the customer efficiently, modification may not be required. But if, for example, customers are driving great distances to obtain your product or service, you should consider some alternatives, like direct mail or new distribution locations.

Promotion is usually the area that undergoes the most changes at the two- to four-year stage. At this stage, you have a better idea of which media to use. But it is important to assess the effectiveness of certain media and determine which advertising works. Evaluate past promotional efforts and make the appropriate changes or modifications. For example, a distributor of bark mulch reviewed her advertising and decided to switch from a large daily paper to smaller, weekly town papers, and as a result the number of inquiries and orders rose 15 percent. In your business, the promotion usually shifts during this time in both the message and the type. The promotional message should change from a focus on the product concept to an emphasis on brand or store preference. For instance, at this stage the distributor of bark mulch should emphasize "Scoffield's Bark Mulch," not just the need for bark mulch generally. Also at this stage you should seek to establish a broad base of loyal customers who will remain in spite of other competitive efforts. If you own a store, you can build this loyalty by sending advance notice of sales and other events to current customers before the general public is notified. You should make customers feel special. Further, you should increase significantly your expenditures and use of newspapers and magazines, with selection based on the product, geographic area, and target market, as you move away from the emphasis on personal selling that you established in earlier stages. Be careful to minimize any wasted exposure. Since sales have been achieved and customers identified, your promotions during this stage should be even more effective.

Maintaining Support Systems

Finally, maintenance of support systems remains important when the business is at this stage. Even though the business is established and is producing sales, you should still seek continued guidance from mentors, a board of directors, and business colleagues. Often at this stage competition becomes a real threat, and therefore advice on marketing mix changes, product or service modification, or customer targeting can be most useful. Trade association involvement can be helpful for determining industry trends and competitive threats. Also, you should continue to keep communication open with family and relatives, making time as needed.

An Established Organization

My business was now eight years old. I realized that we had saturated the local market and that it was time to expand geographically.

This comment by a woman entrepreneur illustrates one characteristic of a business in the five- to ten-year stage. Although most women-owned businesses are less than five years old, many will soon be reaching this next plateau, and women entrepreneurs should be aware of the business characteristics and issues they will encounter next.

Typically, a business reaching five to ten years of age has become profitable and has realized gains and liquidity. Competition exists in what is usually a mature market, and your major concerns are expansion and strategic planning. By this time, you have usually learned to develop adaptive solutions to problems, are confident in your business knowledge of the product, can negotiate with the environment, have delegated some authority, and are learning to plan by systematically assessing costs and benefits. This is in distinct contrast to the situation at start-up when you have to make decisions in the face of continued uncertainty and are very involved in the day-to-day activities of business. The nature of the business at this established stage creates the need to deal with two main issues: expansion and strategic planning.

Expansion

Expansion of any sort, whether geographic or in terms of product or facility, usually requires additional capital. Someone who has guided a business to this stage can certainly consider more financing options than at previous stages. Once again, you must face the debt/equity, control/less control issues. You should make the usual assessment of equity base, amount of present debt, and size of funds needed to select the best source of funds. While bank loans and venture capitalists are always possibilities, depending on the size, growth, and type of product of the enterprise, this may be the time to have a private or public offering of securities of the company. This offering not only infuses capital from many different investors, thereby protecting your control of the business, but it also places a value on the enterprise and provides a mechanism for you to leave the company at a later date. Any placements are of course carefully controlled by the Securities and Exchange Commission, and since the regulations frequently change and must be closely adhered to, you will need outside advice and help.

If no outside equity capital has yet been infused into the firm, it will probably have to be done at this stage if the growth of the company is to be sustained. Venture capitalists, private placement, and public offering are the three primary sources of outside equity capital.

Strategic Planning

The other major issue that you should consider at the five- to ten-year stage is strategic planning. Women entrepreneurs characteristically describe themselves as weak in this area, but this lack is due more to inexperience than to inability. Moreover, since the term *strategic* is often associated with large corporations, it may cause women entrepreneurs to think that they have no need for such planning. In fact, strategic planning is simply a redefinition of the business, an assessment of where the business is now, where it should be, and how to get there. You may ask how the strategic plan is different from a business plan. Simply put, their functions are different. A business plan's primary purpose is to attract investors, secure financing, or provide projections on the viability of the business at start-up or shortly thereafter. A strategic plan, on the other hand, outlines qualitative and quantitative objectives and goals with means for implementation. In this way, it is used as a guide for the company in its growth. One definition of strategic planning describes it as

> the managerial process of developing and maintaining a strategic fit between the organization's goals and capabilities and its changing marketing opportunities. It relies on developing a clear company

mission, supporting objectives and goals, a sound business port-
folio and growth strategy.

Stated in somewhat different terms, it is

the pattern of decision in a company that determines and reveals
its objectives, purposes, goals, produces the principal policies and
plans for achieving those goals, and defines the range of the business the company is to pursue, the kind of economic and non-eco-
nomic contribution it intends to make to its shareholders, employees, customers and communities.[2]

In essence, then, strategic planning is a means of reassessing the
business in its present situation, defining objectives, and implement-
ing changes for continued competitiveness in economically attractive markets.

While many books have been written about strategic planning,
we want to provide you with a basic, useful outline of the process.
The process of strategic planning can be broken down into four
basic steps: determination of objectives, situation analysis, generation and evaluation of alternatives, and strategic plan definition and
implementation.[3] The second step, situation analysis, will require
the most time because it involves assessing the business and its competitive environment in detail.

Step One: Defining Objectives. Defining objectives requires a decision on what the objectives of the firm will be. Generally, a mission
statement or reason for being has already been established in previous analyses, such as the business plan (see chapter 4), but this may
also need to be redefined as the organization grows, as product lines
are expanded, or as markets are modified. The mission statement
should clearly state the purpose of the business, for the objectives of
the business are derived from this mission statement. Unlike the
definition used at the start-up stage, the definition of objectives now
requires more input than just your ideas alone; you should solicit
the ideas of stockholders, the board of directors, lenders, and employees. Objectives are usually stated in terms of activities, and as
such may describe the industries the business is involved in, growth
targets (market share), profitability goals, and cash/investment

trade-offs. These objectives should be used as guideposts for all decisions regarding future directions for the organization. For example, a real estate business may have as its objective "to reach 15 percent market share in our geographic area." For a dress-manufacturing business, the objective may be "to become market leader in producing sequinned evening wear for women."

Step Two: Situation Analysis. The purpose of this step is to develop a clear understanding of where the business currently is and what options are available for the future. The situation analysis should basically evaluate these areas:

Competitive Environment. How is the company doing relative to competition? How intense is the competition?

The Company's Strengths and Weaknesses. How is the company doing economically, in percent share of market, and organizationally? In what areas is the company weak and where does it have an advantage?

Market Structure. Where is the power in the market? How do suppliers, buyers, customers, and substitutes fit in? What are the market segments? Which are the most attractive niches?

Environmental Threats and Opportunities. What role will technology, culture, politics and government, social and demographic changes play in the company's future?

Tools for Analysis. Many tools are available for assessing the present situation, including break-even analysis, market segmentation, and business system analysis. Break-even analysis, discussed in chapter 4, can be a useful tool at this stage for evaluating the cost structure of the business to determine if a cost advantage can be achieved. Likewise, segmentation (also covered in chapter 4) is important in this stage for assessing price sensitivity by customer group, quality requirements, key buying factors in each segment, and delivery expectations. Evaluation of each segment and its characteristics, of the position of the competition in each segment, and of the ability of your business to serve the needs of the targeted segment are all very important.

Business System Analysis. A business system analysis is useful for pointing out the key components of the business system from the time the product is produced to the time it is sold, and assessing the economics of each stage. For instance, the components of a business system in clothing manufacturing typically include designing, cutting, stitching, pressing, and warehousing. You should evaluate each step and determine where the enterprise could possibly achieve a cost advantage, if the system can be changed to improve costs, and how the company's business system compares with other industry participants. This is an important analysis, since cost advantages usually result in higher profits.

In sum, then, a successful situation analysis should provide information on: (1) cost-advantage opportunities, (2) the company's economic structure and changes for improving profitability, (3) market requirements and present effectiveness in meeting the needs and requirements of the customers, (4) relative strengths and weaknesses by product/customer segment, and (5) specific environmental and competitive issues facing the business.

Step Three: Generation and Evaluation of Alternatives. From the information gained through situation analysis, you can identify and detail alternatives. For each alternative, resource requirements and probable results should be noted. An alternative should be selected that is most suitable for the company seeking a sustainable competitive advantage. All conclusions should be clearly documented and responsibilities delineated. At this point, you will have a document to guide your business for the next three to five years and on which you can base decisions. Of course, modifications may be required, depending on changes in the environment, the competition, or the growth of the company.

Step Four: Implementation. The final step in the planning process is to take action and implement the new plan. Individuals should be assigned responsibilities, and specific dates for follow-up should be determined. For example, if the new plan reflects product sales to a new customer group, changes in sales territories or training of new salespeople should commence. A schedule for evaluation at, for instance, three-month or six-month intervals would provide feedback on how the plan is working. To successfully implement the new strategic plan, the company must live up to the new mission statement and achieve the goals set forth. Once this is accomplished, a new plan must be developed.

A Mature Company

A business that has been established ten years or more can be classified as a mature company. At this time the organization undergoes a major overhaul and systems update. There is a search for new products and markets, and price competition is frequently stiff. The woman entrepreneur whose business has survived this long is characteristically goal-oriented, anticipatory in her management; she clearly understands the environment and is up-to-date on the industry and on management techniques. At this stage, too, there are planning issues to consider, as well as a new factor: management succession.

Planning Issues

The planning issues in a mature company revolve around an analysis of the industry and product life cycle. At this stage of the company's growth, at least some of the products are in the mature and declining stage of the product life cycle, as can be seen in figure 7–1. Several strategies are available to help you plan effectively for the

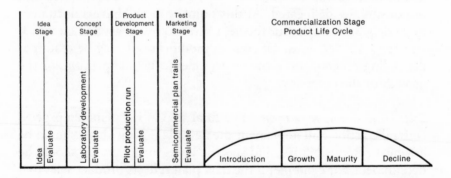

Source: Adapted from Robert D. Hisrich and Michael P. Peters, *Marketing Decisions for New and Mature Products* (Columbus, Ohio: Charles E. Merrill Publishing Co., 1984).

Figure 7–1. *Product-Planning and Development Process*

future: (1) developing and marketing new products; (2) repositioning present products through new market segments, product modification, new uses, or changing marketing mix variables; or (3) selling the business.

Developing and Marketing New Products. The first option, developing and marketing new products, involves a product planning and development process.[4] Beginning with the concept stage and advancing through product development and test marketing, this process helps a firm constantly have new products ready for the market. In order to be effective, evaluation must take place at each stage in the process, reducing the number of new ideas in the first two stages so that maximum time and effort can be spent on fewer ideas. The length of the time period must be carefully weighed in terms of the costs involved in marketing the new idea (commercialization) and the probability of failure.

One of the most difficult tasks in the process is having many new product ideas available. Sources such as customers, competition, distribution channels, the federal government, research and development, and company employees must be constantly monitored for potential ideas. You should then screen these ideas carefully through each of the stages so that time and effort is spent on only the most feasible possibilities.

Repositioning Present Products. The second strategy in the mature stage is to reposition the firm's present products. This objective can be accomplished through new markets, new uses, product modification, or marketing mix modification. The most common error made by women entrepreneurs in this stage of the development of the enterprise is to seek growth of the business through an ever-increasing share of its present market segment. Efforts to do this, however, bring about a competitive response, so that the end result is often the same market positions as before. This strategy is not only difficult, but is usually not very cost-effective either, even where it is possible. You will find it easier, through market segmentation, to identify new national or international market segments.

When new market segments are not available, then perhaps new uses for the product can be developed. These can increase usage among current users, as well as gain new users for the product. A recent example of this strategy is seen in the way that Arm and Hammer repositioned its baking soda by marketing its effectiveness as a deodorizer for refrigerators, a cleaner for swimming pools, and a cleanser for walls. Through this campaign, the company gained significant new sales, and in effect a new life cycle for the product was created.

When new markets or new uses are not available, a product modification or spin-off product can bring about the needed new sales. A.T. Cross introduced the classic black pen to appeal to a market segment that could not afford the higher price of the company's gold and silver pens. Sealtest modified its ice milk in the maturity stage and introduced Sealtest Light 'n' Lively, which helped reposition the product with a good market position. Often by-products of a production process can actually become a new line of products. Annolite Inc., a producer of wooden pallets, started marketing bark mulch for trees and sewers, the mulch a by-product of the pallet production process.

New sales can also be achieved through adjustments in other elements of the marketing mix, such as changing the package, increasing the different quantities or sizes of the offering, increasing the trade discounts, redirecting the promotion with a new, unique selling proposition, or using special consumer or dealer promotions. You may recall how the flip-top can expanded soft-drink sales by producing a convenient package as well as increased exposure in vending machines; or how pouch packs for gravies, sauces, and vegetable and potato products significantly increased sales by appealing to new market segments. In the maturing stage of the company, you should carefully choose marketing strategies that will revitalize the sales and market share of the company in a cost-effective way.

Selling the Business. The final option available to a mature company, selling the business, is frequently employed by women entrepreneurs. Many women entrepreneurs do not enjoy the role of a manager in the enterprise they created. They are interested in doing something new, perhaps starting a new business. Sometimes in order for an enterprise to survive, it is necessary that a new person take over with new ideas, strategy, and vitality. Under these conditions, a buyer for the business should be found who will be able to make the enterprise survive. An inventor falls in love with the invention, an entrepreneur falls in love with the organization, but the love may need to take the form of a sale for the business to survive.

A leveraged buyout is one way for you to sell your business and either start a new one or end your career. If you do not want a lump sum capital gain and/or want to remain with the venture in some capacity, the leveraged buyout may allow a purchaser to acquire the firm under your conditions. You should negotiate the terms of the transaction so that the organizational structure of the enterprise is acceptable and the payment schedule appropriate. The structure and payment schedule are perhaps more important than establishing a mutually acceptable price; nevertheless, the price is important also. Regardless of whether a large or small firm is doing the acquiring, you should insist that a fixed price for the firm be established, not a price contingent on the future performance of the business. Most cases in which women entrepreneurs have received a contingent price have ended in costly legal battles, since of course the woman entrepreneur expects to receive the highest price, and the acquiring firm expects to pay the lowest.

The conditions under which you will run the business following acquisition will be quite different. There will be different controls and reporting procedures once the new management takes over. Standard practices like expensing a family trip, personal use of the company phone, or doing personal business on company time will no longer be standard. In addition, you should understand the problems involved in swapping stock in your company for stock in the large public company. While a stock swap is advantageous for you from an income tax standpoint, it makes the acquiring corporation responsible for any tax liabilities of the acquired business that occur before the sale. Finally, you should be reluctant to give warranties, as is often requested by an acquiring company. Regardless of the status of the business, a warranty makes you legally and financially responsible at a later date. Typical items that are requested to be put under warranty include: no previous violations of the law, no obsolete inventory, and no collectable accounts receivable.

Planning for Succession. Selling the business is one option for planning the business's continuation after you depart, but it is not the only one. Transferring leadership to someone else is another option, though often a difficult one.[5] It can be very hard to relinquish some or all of the decision making to someone else when part of you is woven into every fiber of the business—the blood, sweat, and tears of creating and building a business. Therefore, the most critical factor in successfully handing over the reins of the company to another individual lies in your evaluation of your own desires and future needs. You should determine the extent to which you wish to be involved in the business in the future, the amount of money (if any) you will need from the business in the future, the time available for the succession to take place, and the availability and capability of a successor. There are many options available by which you can successfully transfer leadership, depending on your careful appraisal of these four areas. For example, one woman entrepreneur who wanted to retire completely from the management of the business, but still wanted to conduct research and development, established an independent research and development operation that was completely outside of the day-to-day operations of the business. Regardless of the succession method chosen, you should ensure the continuity of the enterprise by allowing the new leader to make decisions and errors during the training period before the succession and by staying out of the day-to-day decisions of the business if these are the terms of the agreement. Problems frequently occur after the transfer of leadership when the woman entrepreneur cannot totally relinquish the reins. Instead, you should look for a new venture to form or a community service to perform. Perhaps now you will want to devote your time to helping potential woman entrepreneurs succeed as you have—an area that needs all the time you can spare.

The Future for Women Entrepreneurs

It would be nice if women could be brought up the way men are: success-oriented, goal-oriented, and with the understanding it is important to do something with your life.

Schools should create an environment that encourages women to learn finance, focus on careers, and expect to be their own source of financial support.

Stereotypes still exist; women are often typed as secretaries or ad-
ministrative assistants rather than as managers, owners, or CEOs. It
will be easier in the future when these stereotypes are not as strong.

Generally speaking, there has been significant growth in the number of
women-owned businesses in the past twenty-five years, as well as more
opportunities for women in many fields. Today, women entrepreneurs
are more confident, better skilled, and more willing to take risks than
ever before. Unfortunately, there is still a way to go before women entrepreneurs achieve the success of operating a *Fortune* 500 company
and gain complete acceptance in all fields and industries. Although barriers do still come between women and these goals, progress can be
measured in smaller ways, and the future does look promising.

The growth in the number of women-owned businesses has
been increasing at an increasing rate. From 1979 to 1981, the average growth in the number of women-owned businesses per year was
less than 5 percent, whereas from 1981 to 1984 this rate approached
17 percent per year. If we assume a constant 17 percent growth rate
for the next six years, by 1990 the estimated number of women-
owned businesses will grow from 3.5 million to about 9 million.
From a business perspective, this growth will have significant impact because in absolute numbers, women entrepreneurs will not be
so much in a minority; they will comprise much more than the present
5.6 percent of all businesses in the United States. Hence, financial institutions, the government, and industries presently dominated by
men will be more familiar with and accepting of female-owned
businesses, simply because they will no longer seem unusual.

A second important future consideration is the age of the typical
entrepreneurial business owned by a woman. Since most women-
owned businesses are currently young and small, they will experience
significant growth and expansion in the future, and this growth will
help in further establishing the woman entrepreneur in the business
community. At the same time, this maturing of women-owned businesses means that women will have to deal with new and more difficult problems such as expansion, withdrawing mature products from
the market, meeting intense competition, and dealing with declining
markets and products, rising wages, and business reorganization.

The area of social expectations is perhaps the most difficult to
change. Cultural norms assigning women the responsibility for home

and family are in the process of undergoing change, but, even though many men are more accepting of family partnerships, role reversals, and shared household duties, the sex and role stereotypes still remain. Nevertheless, as more women become economically and emotionally independent over the next decade through careers or self-employment, negative attitudes toward women entrepreneurs and their dual roles should diminish in strength. The women entrepreneurs of the late 1960s, the 1970s and the early 1980s are blazing the trail for those who will follow, and perhaps by 1990, the pressure for women entrepreneurs to try to "do it all" will abate, adjustments for family responsibilities and household duties becoming routine rather than exceptions.

There are signs that such changes are now under way. Young women and men today, the entrepreneurs of the future, are being socialized by their parents, schools, and other institutions to realize that they can make their own choices and do not have to follow what society once considered to be typical male- or female-dominated occupations.

> In starting your own business, it's always sink or swim. But in the future, there will be more women succeeding, and they will be role models for younger women. It will be okay to be a successful business or professional person and still be a successful woman. I am optimistic, but realistic about the hard work that entrepreneurship requires.

The women entrepreneurs of the future will not lack confidence or feel that by starting a business they are in an area where they don't belong.

Education will probably help greatly in promoting the future of women entrepreneurs. Positive educational factors include the growth of high school and college courses on small business and entrepreneurship. That educational institutions in general are offering more programs on starting and managing a business creates a more positive environment for women who want to learn business skills.

Once you have successfully established a business, you can contribute to the educational process by participating in high school or college classes as a guest speaker, by hiring students, or by acting as a mentor or role model for a potential woman entrepreneur. This kind of support is invaluable and can create motivation and inspiration for any future woman entrepreneurs.

Because research studies show a lack of solid information on women entrepreneurs, there is a significant effort to learn more about their characteristics and problems. What's more, recent hearings before the U.S. Senate Subcommittee on Small Business have also made clear the need for more data on women-owned businesses. Presumably, as the number of women entrepreneurs grows and as established women-owned businesses continue to succeed, the body of literature for and about women entrepreneurs will also grow.

In all, the future for women entrepreneurs is best described in this comment:

> Real-world experience played a large part in my motivation to achieve. My mother had a career in a day when most women did not even graduate from high school, but it was my father who was the motivator. I have two daughters, one is a sports journalist, the other a strategic planner with a *Fortune* 500 company. I was their motivator.

Appendices

Appendix I
Networks
and Trade Associations

ALASKA

Network
Jean McNeil
Box 25
Iliamna, AK   99606

ARIZONA

American Medical Women's Association
Professional Resources Research Center
Speedway Professional Building,
   Suite 206A
2302 E. Speedway Boulevard
Tuscon, AZ   85719

*Executive Women's Council
of Southern Arizona*
Carolyn Lucz, Chairperson
P.O. Box 44014
Tucson, AZ   85733

WIN (Woman Image Now)
Department of Art
Attn.: Muriel Magenta
Arizona State University
Tempe, AZ   85281

CALIFORNIA

*American Alliance of Women
Entrepreneurs*
c/o Virginia Littlejohn & Associates
2415 Warring St.
Berkeley, CA   94704
(415) 549-0167

Bay Area Executive Women's Forum
356 Urbano
San Francisco, CA   94127
(415) 546-7590

Bay Area Professional Women's Network
55 Sutter St., #329
San Francisco, CA   94101

Embarcadero Center Forum
P.O. Box 2902
San Francisco, CA   94126
(415) 362-3212

American Entrepreneurs Association
3211 Pontius Ave
Los Angeles, CA   90064
(213) 478-0437

*Los Angeles Association of Women
Business Owners*
2410 Beverly Blvd.
Los Angeles, CA   90555
(213) 387-7432

Los Angeles Working Women
Attn: Judy McCullough
304 S. Broadway #534
Los Angeles, CA   90013

*National Federation of Independent
Businesses (NFIB)*
150 W. 20th
San Mateo, CA   94403
(415) 341-7441

The Peninsula Professional Women's Network
701 Welch Rd., Suite 1119
Palo Alto, CA   94303
(415) 328-2040

Professional Women's Networking
Fresno City College
1101 E. University
Fresno, CA   93741
Attn.: Dorothy Sloan

San Francisco Financial Women's Club
808A Spring St.
Sausalito, CA   94965

Tradeswomen, Inc.
P.O. Box 4724
Santa Rosa, CA   95402

Women Can Win!
Attn.: Judy Hochman, President
969 Higard Ave., Suite 603
Los Angeles, CA   90024

Women Entrepreneurs (W.E.)
2030 Union St., Suite 310
San Francisco, CA   94123
(415) 929-0129

Women in Business, Inc.
500 Wilshire Blvd., Suite 1402
Los Angeles, CA   90036
(213) 933-7330

Women in Information and Telecom-munications
109 Minna St., Suite 298
San Francisco, CA   94105
(415) 564-8717

Women's Forum—West
Judith S. Johnson, President
Buttes Gas & Oil Co.
P.O. Box 2071
Oakland, CA   94604

Women's Resource Exchange
35282 Franham Dr.
Newark, CA   94560

COLORADO

Colorado Network of Women's Resource Centers
Better Jobs for Women
1038 Bannock St.
Denver, CO   80204
(303) 893-3534

National Association of Business and Industrial Saleswomen
90 Corona, Suite 1407
Denver, CO   80218
(303) 777-7257

Women Business Owners Association
1557 Ogden
Denver, CO   80202
(303) 832-5418

Women and Business Enterprise
1102 Barberry Ct.
Boulder, CO   80302
(303) 499-6109

Women's Forum of Colorado, Inc
6051 East Dorado Ave.
Englewood, CO   80111
(303) 779-4070

CONNECTICUT

Hartford Women's Network
Hartford Region YWCA
135 Broad St.
Hartford, CT   06105
(203) 525-1163

Mid-day Club
c/o Kane & Von Schmidt
22 West Putnam Ave.
Greenwich, CT   06830

Network of Executive Women
P.O. Box 136
Milford, CT   06460
Contact: Carol Pyke

Network for Professional Women
15 Lewis St.
Hartford, CT   06103
(203) 247-2011

Women in Management
P.O. Box 69
Stamford, CT   06904

DISTRICT OF COLUMBIA

Displaced Homemakers Network
Lower Level B
1325 G St., NW
Washington, D.C.   20005
(202) 628-6767

Federation of Organizations for Professional Women
1825 Connecticut Ave., #403
Washington, D.C.   20009
(202) 328-1415

Mexican-American Women's National Association
1201 16th St., NW, Suite #420
Washington, D.C.   20036
(202) 223-3400

National Action Forum for Older Women
Education and Policy Program
Nancy King, Director
Center for Women's Policy Studies
2000 P St., NW
Washington, D.C.   20036

National Association of Women Business Owners
712 5th St., SE
Washington, D.C.   20003

National Business League
4324 Georgia Ave.
Washington, D.C. 20011
(202) 829-5900

National Council of Career Women
608 H St., SW
Washington, D.C.   20024

National Federation of Business and Professional Women's Clubs
2012 Massachusetts Ave., NW
Washington, D.C.   20036
(202) 293-1100

National Hook-Up of Black Women, Inc.
Shirley Small-Rougeau
1100 Sixth St., NW
Washington, D.C.   20001

National Small Business Association
1604 K St., NW
Washington, D.C.   20006
(202) 296-7400

The Network
c/o Betsy Younkins
American Petroleum Institute
2101 L St., NW
Washington, D.C.   20037

Office of Minority Business Enterprise
U.S. Department of Commerce
Washington, D.C.   20230

Office of Women's Business Enterprise
U.S. Small Business Association
1441 L St., NW
Washington, D.C.   20416

Washington Woman's Network
c/o National Women's Educational
  Foundation
1410 Q St., NW
Washington, D.C.   20004

*Women in Information Processing, Inc.
(WIP)*
P.O. Box 39173
Washington, D.C.   20016
(202) 328-6161

FLORIDA

The Florida Women's Network
P.O. Box 18981
Tampa, FL   18981
(813) 251-9172

Miami Association of Women Business Owners
c/o Caribbean Title Insurance
10871 Caribbean Blvd.
Miami, FL 38189
(305) 251-1447

National Association of Insurance Women
Furlong Insurance Agency
280 NS 42d Ave.
Miami, FL 33126
(305) 446-0832

Women's Information Exchange
Paula Ferrell
Public Relations Director
Center for the Continuing Education
  of Women
Florida Junior College at Jacksonville
101 W. State St.
Jacksonville, FL   32202

GEORGIA

Atlanta Women's Network, Inc.
Ella Alexander, President
P.O. Box 54614
Civic Center Station
Atlanta, GA   30308
(404) 577-5635

Women in Network (WIN)
P.O. Box 1309
Albany, GA   31702
(912) 432-4114

Women's Forum
c/o Beverly Kievman
Marketing Innovations Corp.
P.O. Box 12213
Atlanta, GA   30355

HAWAII

Network of Marketing Women
P.O. Box 27513
Honolulu, HI   96827

ILLINOIS

American Federation of Small Business
407 S. Dearborn St.
Chicago, IL   60605
(312) 427-0207

American Society of Women Accountants
35 E. Wacker Dr.
Chicago, IL   60601

American Women's Society of Certified Public Accountants
5000 N. Michigan Ave., Suite 1400
Chicago, IL   60611
(312) 661-1700

Association of American Women Dentists
211 E. Chicago Ave., 9th Floor
Chicago, IL   60611

Chicago Chapter—National Association of Women Business Owners
500 S. Michigan Ave., Suite 1400
Chicago, IL   60611
(312) 661-1700

Chicago Society of Women Certified Public Accountants
2337 Commonwealth Ave., #1F
Chicago, IL   60614
(312) 525-8887

International Organization of Women Executives
Eileen Galley, President
190 Lockwood Lane
Bloomingdale, IL   60108
(312) 980-4366

National Association of Future Women
805 Plainfield Rd., #216
Darien, IL   60559
(312) 960-2528

The Network of McLean County
1311 Holiday Lane
Bloomington, IL   61701
(309) 662-5506

Woman/Owners/Managers/
Administrators/Networking
(WOMAN)
2520 N. Lincoln Ave., #60
Chicago, IL   60614
Attn.: Anna Benson
(312) 472-8116

Women Employed
5 S. Wabash
Chicago, IL   60603
(312) 782-3902

Women's Council of Realtors
430 N. Michigan Ave.
Chicago, IL   60611
(312) 329-8483

Women's Network
c/o Sandra M. Traicoff
912 Shoreline
Dunlap, IL   61525

INDIANA

The Network of Women in Business
9331 N. Washington Blvd.
Indianapolis, IN   46240
(317) 844-8503

NWS Women's Network
Sandra Stepler-Hajtonk
627 W. U.S. 30
Valparaiso, IN   46383

IOWA

Nexus (Executive Women's Alliance)
c/o Betsy Bowles
Penguin Studio
1005 Insurance Exchange Building
Des Moines, IA   50309

KENTUCKY

Women's Chamber of Commerce of
Kentucky
Marie Humphries
P.O. Box 35561
Louisville, KY   40232

LOUISIANA

Network
P.O. Box 3081
Baton Rouge, LA   70821

Women Professionals in Petroleum
3203 Memorial Park Dr., #75
New Orleans, LA   70114
(504) 521-5319

MARYLAND

Association for Women in Computing, Inc.
407 Hillmoor Dr.
Silver Spring, MD   20901

Baltimore Executive Women's Network
Sally Feimer
Baltimore New Directions for Women
2517 N. Charles St.
Baltimore, MD   21218

Executive Women's Council, Greater
Baltimore
c/o Eastford Professional Services
304 W. Chesapeake Ave.
Towson, MD   21204
(301) 825-7841

National Women's Studies Association
Elaine Reuben, Coordinator
University of Maryland
College Park, MD   20742

Women Managers
Carol Parr
10302 E. Nolcrest Dr.
Silver Spring, MD   20903

MASSACHUSETTS

Boston Luncheon Club
c/o Deane C. Laycock
Trust Officer, Fiduciary Trust
P.O. Box 1647
Boston, MA   02105
(617) 482-5270

Coalition of Women in National and
International Business
P.O. Box 950
Boston, MA   02119
(617) 793-7388

*The National Alliance of Professional
and Executive Women's Networks*
Deane C. Laycock, Executive Director
1 Faneuil Hall Marketplace
Boston, MA   02109
(617) 720-2874

Network
Evergreen Realty
140 South St.
Pittsfield, MA   02101
Contact: Myrna Hammerling
(413) 499-4610

Small Business Association of New England
69 Hickory Dr.
Waltham, MA   02157
(617) 890-9070

*West Suburban Area Women's Network
Group*
Middlesex Community College
P.O. Box T
Bedford, MA   01730

Women/West and Women/South of Boston
31 Stonebridge Road
Wayland, MA   01778
(617) 653-7867

Women's Lunch Group
c/o 760 Associates
35 Wykeham Road
West Newton, MA   02165
(617) 969-3678

Women's Network Exchange
140 Clarendon St.
Boston, MA   02109
Publishes a directory,
Keep Connected (for Greater Boston
   area), $4.95
(617) 247-1835

MICHIGAN

Detroit Women's Forum
c/o American Jewish Committee
163 Madison
Detroit, MI   48226
(313) 965-3353

MINNESOTA

All the Good Old Girls
The Minnesota Women's Network
640 East Grant
Minneapolis, MN   55404
(612) 375-9496

All the Good Old Girls
Rochester Community College
Consortium Office, Room 1223
Rochester, MN   55901
(507) 285-7275

MISSOURI

American Business Women's Association
National Headquarters
9100 Ward Parkway
P.O. Box 8728
Kansas City, MO   64114
(816) 361-6621

*National Association of Minority Women
in Business*
City Square Center
P.O. Box 26412
Kansas City, MO   64169
(816) 421-3335

Women in Business Network
Ralston Purina Company
Checkerboard Square 6T
St. Louis, MO   63188

MONTANA

Focus on Women
Montana State University
Bozeman, MT   59717

*Montana Association for Female
Executives, Inc.*
2423 Pine Street
Billings, MT   59101
(406) 252-6512

NEBRASKA

Association of Independent Business Women
c/o Byron Reed Co., Inc.
600 Continental Building
Omaha, NB   68102
Contact: Donna Hanson
(402) 342-8100

Omaha Network
c/o Marlene Hansen
Hansen & Hansen
1905 Harney
Omaha, NB   68102

NEW JERSEY

*National Alliance for Homebased Business
Women*
P.O. Box 306
Midland Park, NJ   07432

South Jersey Business Women's Network
c/o Donna Caffrey
RD 3, Memory Lane
Folsom, NJ   08038
(609) 561-0182

NEW MEXICO

The Association
c/o Lewis Limited
Box 3009
Las Cruces, NM   88003
(505) 522-8032

NEW YORK

Advertising Women of New York
153 E. 57th Street
New York, NY   10022

Albany Women's Forum
c/o Jan Beesmeyer
Executive Director, Albany YWCA
28 Colvin Avenue
Albany, NY   12205
(518) 438-6608

American Management Association
135 W. 50th Street
New York, NY   10020

*American Medical Women's Association,
Inc.*
465 Grand St.
New York, NY   10002
(212) 533-5104

*Association of Business and Professional
Women in Construction*
331 Madison Avenue
New York, NY   10017

Catalyst
14 E. 60th Street
New York, NY   10022
(212) 759-9700

Financial Women's Association
P.O. Box 1605
1 Bankers Trust Plaza
New York, NY   10185
(212) 764-6476

*The Fortune 500—Business and Profes-
sional Women's Club*
150 W. 52d Street
New York, NY   10019
(212) 868-3330

Long Island Women's Network
Phyllis S. Vineyard
10 S. Brewster Lane
Bellport, NY   11713

*New York Association of Women
Business Owners*
150 W. 52nd St.
New York, NY   10020
(212) 245-8230

*The New York Women's Bar
Association*
c/o Linda Lamel
New York State Insurance Department
2 World Trade Center
New York, NY   10047
(212) 488-4122

*One Ten Center for Business and Profes-
sional Women*
(Nonprofit Networking Association)
P.O. Box 327
Mineola, NY   11501

Organization of Women Professionals
c/o Avriel Goldberger
Hofstra University
Hempstead, NY   11550

Presidents Association
135 W. 50th Street
New York, NY   10020

Professional Women's Network
18 Newton Avenue
Norwich, NY   13815
Gina Potter, President
(607) 334-3218

Rochester Women's Network
c/o Women's Career Center, Inc.
121 N. Fitzhugh Street
Rochester, NY   14614
(716) 325-6165

Rockland County Women's Network
c/o Rockland Community College
145 College Road
Suffern, NY   10901
(914) 356-4650

*Westchester Association of Women
Business Owners*
25 Bellwood Road
White Plains, NY   10603
(914) 592-3188

Women's Economic Round Table
860 United Nations Plaza
New York, NY   10017
(212) 759-4360

Women's Forum, Inc.,
221 E. 71st Street
New York, NY   10021
(212) 535-9840

Women's Network
c/o YWCA of Binghamton and Broome
   County
Hawley and Exchange Streets
Binghamton, NY   13901
(607) 772-0340

Women's Network of Fifth Avenue
7 W. 55th Street
New York, NY   10019

The Young Presidents Organization (YPO)
52 Vanderbilt Ave.
New York, NY   10017
(212) 867-1900

NORTH CAROLINA

New Girls Network
Director of Continuing Education
Salem College
Winston-Salem, NC   27108

Women Executives
5842 McNair Road
Charlotte, NC   28212

OHIO

National Association of Working Women
1224 Huron Rd.
Cleveland, OH   44115
(216) 566-9308

Women's Career Network Associatic
106 E. Bridge Street
Berea, OH   44017

The Women's Network
People's Federal Savings
39 E. Market Street
Akron, OH   44308

OKLAHOMA

American Business Women's Association
c/o Alnoma E. Dinger
Southwestern Bell
P.O. Box 1380
Tulsa, OK   74121
(918) 585-6250

National Association of Insurance Women
1847 E. 15th Street
P.O. Box 4694
Tulsa, OK   74104

Women Executives Network
c/o Linda J. Daxon
Oklahoma City Chamber of Commerce
One Santa Fe Plaza
Oklahoma City, OK   73133
(405) 232-6381

OREGON

Institute for Managerial and Professional Women
1979 SW Fifth Avenue
Portland, OR   97201
(503) 226-7701
Eugene branch:
P.O. Box 3815
Eugene, OR   97403

International Network of Business and Professional Women
6424 NE Mallory
Portland, OR   97211
(503) 289-0400

PENNSYLVANIA

Division for Women in Medicine
The Medical College of Pennsylvania
3300 Henry Avenue
Philadelphia, PA   19129

Executive Women's Council, Greater Pittsburgh
2 Gateway Center
Pittsburgh, PA   15222
(412) 355-0805

The Woman's Network
325 West Avenue
Wayne, PA   19087
(215) 687-9485

TEXAS

National Association of Minority Entrepreneurs
501 Wynnewood Village
Dallas, TX   75223
(214) 941-4246

National Association of Women in Construction
327 S. Adams
Fort Worth, TX   76104
(817) 877-5551

Network for Executive Women
Peg Knapp
1203 Lake Street, Suite 214
Fort Worth, TX   76102
(817) 332-6329

Women Entrepreneur's Association
3610 Pioneer Parkway
Dallas, TX   75215
(214) 461-6488

VIRGINIA

Peninsula Women's Network
Christopher Newport College
P.O. Box 6070
Newport News, VA   23606
(804) 599-7153

WASHINGTON

American Society of Women Accountants
5646 37th Avenue, SW
Seattle, WA   98126

Executive Women International
Mrs. Lou Jensen
500 Wall Street, Suite #410
Seattle, WA   98121

Institute for Managerial and Professional Women
P.O. Box 3931
Bellevue, WA   98009

NW Women's Law Center
701 E. Northlake Place
Seattle, WA   98105
(206) 632-8468

Seattle Women in Advertising
Virginia Landree
KSTW-TV
P.O. Box 11411
Tacoma, WA   98411

Seattle Society of Women Engineers
Pacific Northwest Section
c/o C. Noah-Nichols
25812 SW Tiger Mountain Road
Issaquah, WA   98027

Soroptimist International—Seattle
P.O. Box 2676
Seattle, WA   98111

Women's Business Exchange
Donna Nunn
314 Lloyd Building
6th and Steward
Seattle, WA   98101

Women's Network
1107 E. Olive Street
Seattle, WA   98101
(206) 323-6490

WISCONSIN

International Council for Small Business
c/o Robert D. Banes
University of Wisconsin, Ext.
929 N. 6th Street
Milwaukee, WI   53202
(414) 224-1818

Wisconsin Women's Network
625 W. Washington Avenue
Madison, WI   53703

Women in Self-Employment
c/o 317 W. Johnson Street
Madison, WI   53703
(608) 257-7888

CANADA

Edmonton Women's Network
c/o Lana B. Black
10310 137th Street
Edmonton, Alberta, Canada   T5N 2H1
(403) 454-7026 (evenings)

Vancouver Women's Network
Center for Continuing Education
The University of British Columbia
Vancouver, Canada   V6T 1W5
(604) 228-2181

Appendix II
Information Sources
for the Woman Entrepreneur

BOOKS

Abell, Derek F., and John S. Hammond. *Strategic Market Planning.* Englewood Cliffs, N.J.: Prentice-Hall, 1979.

Baty, George. *Entrepreneurship for the Eighties.* Englewood Cliffs, N.J.: Prentice-Hall, 1981.

Baumback, Clifford M., K. Lawyer, and P.D. Kelley. *How to Organize and Operate a Small Business.* Englewood Cliffs, N.J.: Prentice-Hall, 1979.

Barge, David. *Patents and Trademark Tactics and Practice.* (New York: John Wiley and Sons, 1980.

Danco, Leon. *Beyond Survival.* 5th ed. Cleveland, Ohio: The University Press, 1979.

Danco, Leon. *Inside the Family Business.* Cleveland Ohio: The University Press, 1980.

Fisher, Roger, and William Ury. *Getting to Yes: Negotiating Agreement Without Giving In.* New York: Penguin Books, 1983.

Gross, Harry. *Financing for Small and Medium Size Businesses.* Englewood Cliffs, N.J.: Prentice-Hall, 1969.

Hancock, William. *The Small Business Legal Advisor.* New York: McGraw-Hill Book Co., 1982.

Henke, Russel W. *Effective R & D for the Smaller Company.* Houston: Gulf Publishing Co., 1963.

Hennig, Margaret, and Anne Jardim. *The Management Woman.* (New York: Double-day, Anchor Press, 1971.

Herbert, Robert F., and Albert N. Link. *The Entrepreneur—Mainstream Views and Radical Critiques.* New York: Praeger Publishing Co., 1982.

Hisrich, Robert D., and John J. McNamara. *Marketing: A Practical Managerial Approach.* St. Paul, Minn.: West Publishing Co., 1985.

Hisrich, Robert D., and Michael P. Peters. *Marketing Decisions for New and Mature Products.* Columbus, Ohio: Charles E. Merrill Publishing Co., 1984.

Huang, Stanley. *Investment Analysis and Management*. Cambridge, Mass.: Winthrop Publishers, 1981.

Jain, Subhash C. *Marketing and Planning Strategy*. Cincinnati, Ohio: Southwestern Publishing Co., 1981.

Kennedy, Gavin, John Benson, and John McMillan. *Managing Negotiations*. London: Business Books Ltd., 1980.

Kruzas, Anthony T., and Robert C. Thomas, eds. *Business Organizations and Agencies Directory*. 1st ed. Detroit, Mich.: Gale Research Company, 1980.

Lane, Marc J. *Legal Handbook for Small Business*. New York: AMACOM, 1977.

McGowan, Judith. *Inc. Yourself: How to Profit by Setting Up Your Own Corporation*. New York: Macmillan, 1977.

Porter, Michael P. *Competitive Strategy Techniques for Analyzing Industry and Competitors*. New York: The Free Press, 1980.

Pratt, Stanley E., ed. *Guide to Venture Capital Sources*. 7th ed. Wellesley, Mass.: Capital Publishing Co., 1983.

Raiffa, Howard. *The Art and Science of Negotiation*. Cambridge: Harvard University Press, 1982.

Rohrlich, Chester. *Organizing Corporate and Other Business Enterprises*. New York: Matthew Bender Co., 1975.

Ronstadt, Robert C. *Entrepreneurship Text, Cases, and Notes*. Dover, Mass.: Lord Publishing Co., 1984.

Simon, Julian. *How to Start and Operate a Mail Order Business*. New York: McGraw-Hill Book., 1981.

Steinhoff, Dan. *Small Business Management Fundamentals*. 3rd ed. New York: McGraw-Hill Book Co., 1982.

Still, Jack W. *A Guide to Managerial Accounting in Small Companies*. (Englewood Cliffs, N.J.: Prentice-Hall, 1969.

Tate, Curtis E., Leon C. Megginson, Charles R. Scott, and Lyle R. Trueblood. *Successful Small Business Management*. Dallas, Tex.: Business Publications, 1982.

Timmons, Jeffrey, Leonard E. Smollen, and Alelxander Dingee. *New Venture Creation: A Guide to Small Business Development*. Wellesley, Mass.: Capital Publishing Co., 1983.

Vesper, Karl H. *New Venture Strategies*. Englewood Cliffs, N.J.: Prentice-Hall, 1980.

Welch, Mary Scott. *Networking*. New York: Warner Books, published by arrangement with Harcourt Brace Jovanich, 1981.

Winston, Sandra. *The Entrepreneurial Woman*. New York: Newsweek Books, 1977.

PERIODICALS

Advertising Age
Administrative Science Quarterly
Business Week

California Management Review
Dun's
Financial Analysts Journal
Forbes
Fortune
Harvard Business Review
Inc. Magazine
Journal of Small Business Management
Management Review
Marketing News
Nation's Business
Venture
Venture Capital Journal
Wall Street Journal

OTHER

A Directory of Federal Government Business Assistance Programs for Women Business Owners. Washington, D.C.: Small Business Association, 1980.
A Guide to the United States Department of Commerce for Women Business Owners. Washington, D.C.: Department of Commerce, January 1980.
Resource Groups for Women in Business. Washington, D.C.: Center for Women's Policy Studies, 1971.

Appendix III
Pro Forma Statements

	Year 1	Year 2	Year 3
Sales			
Less: Cost of Goods Sold			
Gross profit			
Operating expenses:			
Outside labor			
Operating supplies			
Salaries, wages, & commissions			
Repairs and maintenance			
Advertising & promotion			
Delivery			
Bad debts			
General office administration			
Rent			
Utilities			
Insurance			
Taxes			
Interest			
Depreciation			
Miscellaneous			
Total operating expenses			
Profit (loss) pretax			
Taxes			
Net profit (loss)			

Figure III–1. *Pro Forma Income Statement—Three-Year Summary*

	July 19___	Aug. 19___	Sept. 19___	Oct. 19___	Total
Sales	___	___	___	___	___
Less: Cost of Goods Sold	___	___	___	___	___
Gross profit					
Operating expenses:					
Outside labor	___	___	___	___	___
Operating supplies	___	___	___	___	___
Salaries, wages, & commissions	___	___	___	___	___
Repairs & maintenance	___	___	___	___	___
Advertising & promotion	___	___	___	___	___
Delivery	___	___	___	___	___
Bad debts	___	___	___	___	___
General office administration	___	___	___	___	___
Rent	___	___	___	___	___
Utilities	___	___	___	___	___
Insurance	___	___	___	___	___
Taxes	___	___	___	___	___
Interest	___	___	___	___	___
Depreciation	___	___	___	___	___
Miscellaneous	___	___	___	___	___
Total operating expenses	___	___	___	___	___
Profit (loss) pretax	___	___	___	___	___
Taxes	___	___	___	___	___
Net profit (loss)	___	___	___	___	___

Figure III–2. *Pro Forma Income Statement—First Year, by Month*

	Year 2 1st Qtr.	Year 2 2nd Qtr.	Year 2 3rd Qtr.	Year 2 4th Qtr.	Total
Sales	_____	_____	_____	_____	_____
Less: Cost of Goods Sold	_____	_____	_____	_____	_____
Gross profit					
Operating expenses:					
Outside labor	_____	_____	_____	_____	_____
Operating supplies	_____	_____	_____	_____	_____
Salaries, wages, & commissions	_____	_____	_____	_____	_____
Repairs & maintenance	_____	_____	_____	_____	_____
Advertising & promotion	_____	_____	_____	_____	_____
Delivery	_____	_____	_____	_____	_____
Bad debts	_____	_____	_____	_____	_____
General office administration	_____	_____	_____	_____	_____
Rent	_____	_____	_____	_____	_____
Utilities	_____	_____	_____	_____	_____
Insurance	_____	_____	_____	_____	_____
Taxes	_____	_____	_____	_____	_____
Interest	_____	_____	_____	_____	_____
Depreciation	_____	_____	_____	_____	_____
Miscellaneous	_____	_____	_____	_____	_____
Total operating expenses	_____	_____	_____	_____	_____
Profit (loss) pretax	_____	_____	_____	_____	_____
Taxes	_____	_____	_____	_____	_____
Net profit (loss)	_____	_____	_____	_____	_____

Figure III–3. *Pro Forma Income Statement—Second Year, by Quarter*

	Year 3 1st Qtr.	Year 3 2nd Qtr.	Year 3 3rd Qtr.	Year 3 4th Qtr.	Year 3 Total
Sales	_____	_____	_____	_____	_____
Less: Cost of Goods Sold	_____	_____	_____	_____	_____
Gross profit					
Operating expenses:					
Outside labor	_____	_____	_____	_____	_____
Operating supplies	_____	_____	_____	_____	_____
Salaries, wages, & commissions	_____	_____	_____	_____	_____
Repairs & main- tenance	_____	_____	_____	_____	_____
Advertising & pro- motion	_____	_____	_____	_____	_____
Car	_____	_____	_____	_____	_____
Bad debts	_____	_____	_____	_____	_____
General office administration	_____	_____	_____	_____	_____
Rent	_____	_____	_____	_____	_____
Utilities	_____	_____	_____	_____	_____
Insurance	_____	_____	_____	_____	_____
Taxes	_____	_____	_____	_____	_____
Interest	_____	_____	_____	_____	_____
Depreciation	_____	_____	_____	_____	_____
Miscellaneous	_____	_____	_____	_____	_____
Total operating expenses	_____	_____	_____	_____	_____
Profit (loss) pretax	_____	_____	_____	_____	_____
Taxes	_____	_____	_____	_____	_____
Net profit (loss)	_____	_____	_____	_____	_____

Figure III–4. *Pro Forma Income Statement—Third Year, by Quarter*

	Year 1	Year 2	Year 3
Cash receipts			
Sales			
Retail	_____	_____	_____
Wholesale	_____	_____	_____
Other	_____	___ ___	_____
Other cash receipts	_____	_____	_____
Total cash receipts	_____	_____	_____
Cash disbursements:			
Cost of goods	_____	_____	_____
Outside labor	_____	_____	_____
Operating supplies	_____	_____	_____
Salaries, wages, & commis- sions	_____	_____	_____
Repairs and maintenance	_____	_____	_____
Advertising & promotion	_____	_____	_____
Car	_____	_____	_____
Bad debts	_____	_____	_____
General office administration	_____	_____	_____
Rent	_____	_____	_____
Utilities	_____	_____	_____
Insurance	_____	_____	_____
Taxes	_____	_____	_____
Interest	_____	_____	_____
Loan principal	_____	_____	_____
Miscellaneous	_____	_____	_____
Total cash disbursements	_____	_____	_____
Net cash flow	_____	_____	_____
Cumulative cash flow	_____	_____	_____

Figure III–5. *Pro Forma Cash Flow—Three-Year Summary*

	July 19___	Aug. 19___	Sept. 19___	Oct. 19___	Total
Cash receipts:					
Sales:					
Retail	_____	_____	_____	_____	_____
Wholesale	_____	_____	_____	_____	_____
Other	_____	_____	_____	_____	_____
Other cash receipts	_____	_____	_____	_____	_____
Total cash receipts	_____	_____	_____	_____	_____
Cash disbursements:					
Cost of goods	_____	_____	_____	_____	_____
Outside labor	_____	_____	_____	_____	_____
Operating supplies	_____	_____	_____	_____	_____
Salaries, wages, & commissions	_____	_____	_____	_____	_____
Repairs & maintenance	_____	_____	_____	_____	_____
Advertising & promotion	_____	_____	_____	_____	_____
Car	_____	_____	_____	_____	_____
Bad debts	_____	_____	_____	_____	_____
General office administration	_____	_____	_____	_____	_____
Rent	_____	_____	_____	_____	_____
Utilities	_____	_____	_____	_____	_____
Insurance	_____	_____	_____	_____	_____
Taxes	_____	_____	_____	_____	_____
Interest	_____	_____	_____	_____	_____
Loan principal	_____	_____	_____	_____	_____
Miscellaneous	_____	_____	_____	_____	_____
Total cash disbursements	_____	_____	_____	_____	_____
Net cash flow	_____	_____	_____	_____	_____
Cumulative cash flow	_____	_____	_____	_____	_____

Figure III–6. *Pro Forma Cash Flow—First Year, by Month*

	Year 2 1st Qtr.	Year 2 2nd Qtr.	Year 2 3rd Qtr.	Year 2 4th Qtr.	Total
Cash receipts:					
Sales:					
Retail	_____	_____	_____	_____	_____
Wholesale	_____	_____	_____	_____	_____
Other	_____	_____	_____	_____	_____
Other cash receipts	_____	_____	_____	_____	_____
Total cash receipts	_____	_____	_____	_____	_____
Cash disbursements:					
Cost of goods	_____	_____	_____	_____	_____
Outside labor	_____	_____	_____	_____	_____
Operating supplies	_____	_____	_____	_____	_____
Salaries, wages, & commissions	_____	_____	_____	_____	_____
Repairs & maintenance	_____	_____	_____	_____	_____
Advertising & promotion	_____	_____	_____	_____	_____
Car	_____	_____	_____	_____	_____
Bad debts	_____	_____	_____	_____	_____
General office administration	_____	_____	_____	_____	_____
Rent	_____	_____	_____	_____	_____
Utilities	_____	_____	_____	_____	_____
Insurance	_____	_____	_____	_____	_____
Taxes	_____	_____	_____	_____	_____
Interest	_____	_____	_____	_____	_____
Loan principal	_____	_____	_____	_____	_____
Miscellaneous	_____	_____	_____	_____	_____
Total cash disbursements	_____	_____	_____	_____	_____
Net cash flow	_____	_____	_____	_____	_____
Cumulative cash flow	_____	_____	_____	_____	_____

Figure III–7. *Pro Forma Cash Flow—Second Year, by Quarter*

	Year 3 1st Qtr.	Year 3 2nd Qtr.	Year 3 3rd Qtr.	Year 3 4th Qtr.	Total
Cash receipts:					
Sales:					
Retail	_____	_____	_____	_____	_____
Wholesale	_____	_____	_____	_____	_____
Other	_____	_____	_____	_____	_____
Other cash receipts	_____	_____	_____	_____	_____
Total cash receipts	_____	_____	_____	_____	_____
Cash disbursements:					
Cost of goods	_____	_____	_____	_____	_____
Outside labor	_____	_____	_____	_____	_____
Operating supplies	_____	_____	_____	_____	_____
Salaries, wages, & commissions	_____	_____	_____	_____	_____
Repairs & maintenance	_____	_____	_____	_____	_____
Advertising & promotion	_____	_____	_____	_____	_____
Car	_____	_____	_____	_____	_____
Bad debts	_____	_____	_____	_____	_____
General office administration	_____	_____	_____	_____	_____
Rent	_____	_____	_____	_____	_____
Utilities	_____	_____	_____	_____	_____
Insurance	_____	_____	_____	_____	_____
Taxes	_____	_____	_____	_____	_____
Interest	_____	_____	_____	_____	_____
Loan principal	_____	_____	_____	_____	_____
Miscellaneous	_____	_____	_____	_____	_____
Total cash disbursements	_____	_____	_____	_____	_____
Net cash flow	_____	_____	_____	_____	_____
Cumulative cash flow	_____	_____	_____	_____	_____

Figure III–8. *Pro Forma Cash Flow—Third Year, by Quarter*

	A Actual for Month	B Budget for Month	C Deviation B − A	D % Deviation $\dfrac{C}{B} \times 100$
Month: _____				
Sales				
Less: Cost of Goods Sold	_____	_____	_____	_____
Gross profit	_____	_____	_____	_____
Operating expenses:				
Outside labor	_____	_____	_____	_____
Operating supplies	_____	_____	_____	_____
Salaries, wages, & commissions	_____	_____	_____	_____
Repairs & maintenance	_____	_____	_____	_____
Advertising & promotion	_____	_____	_____	_____
Car	_____	_____	_____	_____
Bad debts	_____	_____	_____	_____
General office administration	_____	_____	_____	_____
Rent	_____	_____	_____	_____
Utilities	_____	_____	_____	_____
Insurance	_____	_____	_____	_____
Taxes	_____	_____	_____	_____
Interest	_____	_____	_____	_____
Depreciation	_____	_____	_____	_____
Miscellaneous	_____	_____	_____	_____
Total operating expenses	_____	_____	_____	_____
Profit (loss) pretax	_____	_____	_____	_____
Taxes	_____	_____	_____	_____
Net profit (loss)	_____	_____	_____	_____

Figure III–9. *Budget Deviation Analysis—Income Statement*

| | Month: _____ | | | |
	A Actual for Month	B Budget for Month	C Deviation B − A	D % Deviation $\frac{C}{B} \times 100$
Beginning cash balance	_____	_____	_____	_____
Add: sales				
Retail	_____	_____	_____	_____
Wholesale	_____	_____	_____	_____
Other	_____	_____	_____	_____
Other cash receipts	_____	_____	_____	_____
Total cash receipts	_____	_____	_____	_____
Deduct: cash disbursements				
Cost of goods	_____	_____	_____	_____
Outside labor	_____	_____	_____	_____
Operating supplies	_____	_____	_____	_____
Salaries, wages, & commissions	_____	_____	_____	_____
Repairs & maintenance	_____	_____	_____	_____
Advertising & promotion	_____	_____	_____	_____
Car	_____	_____	_____	_____
Bad debts	_____	_____	_____	_____
General office administration	_____	_____	_____	_____
Rent	_____	_____	_____	_____
Utilities	_____	_____	_____	_____
Insurance	_____	_____	_____	_____
Taxes	_____	_____	_____	_____
Interest	_____	_____	_____	_____
Loan principal	_____	_____	_____	_____
Miscellaneous	_____	_____	_____	_____
Total cash disbursements	_____	_____	_____	_____
Net cash flow	_____	_____	_____	_____
Cumulative cash flow	_____	_____	_____	_____

Figure III–10. *Budget Deviation Analysis—Cash Flow*

Notes

CHAPTER 1

1. Robert F. Hebert and Albert N. Link, *The Entrepreneur—Mainstream Views and Radical Critiques* (New York: Praeger Publishing, 1982), 17.
2. Joseph Schumpeter, *Can Capitalism Survive?* (New York: Harper and Row, 1952), 72.
3. Karl Vesper, *New Venture Strategies* (Englewood Cliffs, N.J.: Prentice-Hall, Inc., 1980), 2.
4. These and other factors are discussed in: Sandra Winston, *The Entrepreneurial Woman* (New York: Newsweek Books, 1979).
5. Sookie Stambler, *Women's Liberation—Blueprint for the Future* (New York: Ace Books, 1970), 267.
6. Eleanor B. Schwartz, "Entrepreneurship: A New Female Frontier," *Journal of Contemporary Business* (Winter 1979): 47–76.
7. James DeCarlo and Paul R. Lyons, "A Comparison of Selected Personal Characteristics of Minority and Non-Minority Female Entrepreneurs," *Journal of Small Business Management* (December 1979):22–29.
8. Robert D. Hisrich and Marie O'Brien, "The Woman Entrepreneur from a Business and Sociological Perspective," *Frontiers of Entrepreneurship Research, 1981* (Proceedings of the 1981 Conference on Entrepreneurship, Babson College, June 1981), 21–39.
9. Robert D. Hisrich and Marie O'Brien, "The Woman Entrepreneur as a Reflection of the Type of Business," *Frontiers of Entrepreneurship Research, 1982* (Proceedings of the 1982 Conference on Entrepreneurship, Babson College, June 1982), 54–67.
10. Robert D. Hisrich and Candida Brush, "The Woman Entrepreneur: Management Skills and Business Problems," *Journal of Small Business Management* (January 1984):30–37.

CHAPTER 3

1. Margaret Hennig and Anne Jardim, *The Managerial Woman* (New York: Doubleday, Anchor Press, 1971), 178.
2. Senate Committee on Small Business, *Hearings on Women Entrepreneurs: Their Success and Problems,* 98th Cong., 2nd sess., 30 May 1984, 18.

CHAPTER 4

1. *Senate Select Committee on Small Business, Small Business Administration Contract Procurement Program,* 95th Cong., 1st sess., 1977, 67.
2. U.S. Department of Commerce, *The Bottom-Line: Unequal Enterprise in America,* Report of the President's Interagency Task Force on Women Business Owners (Washington, D.C.: Government Printing Office, 1978), 7.
3. "Women Chief Executives Help Each Other with Frank Advice," *Wall Street Journal,* Small Business Column, 2 July 1984, p. 21.
4. For a thorough discussion of business plans and particular market plans see Derek F. Abell and John S. Hammond, *Strategic Market Planning* (Englewood Cliffs, N.J.: Prentice-Hall, Inc., 1979).
5. These are based on a survey of 267 companies. See John Hopkins, *The Marketing Plan* (New York: The Conference Board, Inc., 1981), 2.
6. For a complete discussion of competitive analyses, see Michael E. Porter, *Competitive Strategy Techniques for Analyzing Industry and Competitors* (New York: The Free Press, 1980).
7. A discussion of these and other corporate structures can be found in Marc Lane, *A Legal Handbook for Non-profit Organizations* (New York: AMACOM, 1980).
8. For a discussion of the process and costs in each of the states, see Judith McGowan, *Inc. Yourself: How to Profit by Setting Up Your Own Corporation* (New York: Macmillan, 1980).
9. A discussion of this can be found in "Taking the S-Corporation Route to Tax Savings," *Inc. Magazine,* December 1983, 160–72.

CHAPTER 5

1. These sources of capital are developed thoroughly in a book by Robert C. Ronstadt, *Entrepreneurship Text, Cases, and Notes,* (Dover, Mass.: Lord Publishing Co., 1984), 645–58.
2. For a discussion of private placements, see William Wetzel, "Informal Risk Capital in New England," *Proceedings,* 1981 Conference on Entrepreneurship (June, 1981), 210–24; and Robert Ronstadt, *Entrepreneurship* (Dover, Mass.: Lord Publishing Co., 1984), 683–700.
3. This is discussed in Robert T. Jarvis, "Starting a Small Business: An Investigation of the Borrowing Procedure," *Journal of Small Business Management* (October 1982):22–31.

4. Sources for this information include Dun and Bradstreet's *Financial Ratios;* NCR's *Expenses;* and Robert Norris Associates' *Annual Statement Studies.*
5. Len Fertuck, "Survey of Small Business Lending Practices," *Journal of Small Business Management* (October 1982):32–41.
6. Ibid.
7. Mary Scott Welch, *Networking* (New York: Warner Books, 1981), 27.
8. Adapted from Welch, *Networking*, 81–123.

CHAPTER 6

1. These steps are thoroughly discussed in Gavin Kennedy, John Benson, and John McMillan, *Managing Negotiations* (London: Basic Books Ltd., 1980), 18–115.
2. For further information, see Peter F. Drucker, *The Effective Executive* (New York: Harper and Row, 1966), 35.
3. Adapted from Larry D. Redinbaugh and Clyde W. Neu, *Small Business Management—A Planning Approach* (St. Paul, Minn.: West Publishing Co., 1980), 427–29.

CHAPTER 7

1. Philip Kotler, *Principles of Marketing,* 2d ed., (Englewood Cliffs, N.J.: Prentice-Hall, 1983), 515.
2. Kenneth B. Andrews, *The Concept of Corporate Strategy* (Homewood, Ill.: Richard D. Irwin, 1980), 15.
3. See also George A. Steiner, "Approaches to Long-Range Planning for Small Businesses," in *Entrepreneurship and Venture Management,* ed. Clifford M. Baumback and Joseph R. Mancuso (Englewood Cliffs, N.J.: Prentice-Hall, 1975), 160–79.
4. For an in-depth presentation of this process, see Robert D. Hisrich and Michael P. Peters, *Marketing Decisions for New and Mature Products* (Columbus, Ohio: Charles E. Merrill Publishing Co., 1984).
5. A complete discussion of planning for succession can be found in Robert C. Ronstadt, *Entrepreneurship* (Dover, Mass.: Lord Publishing Co., 1984), 745–60; Stanley Davis, "Entrepreneurial Succession," *Administrative Science Quarterly* (December 1967); and Harry Levinson, "Conflicts that Plague Family Businesses," *Harvard Business Review* (March/April, 1971).

Glossary

Acid test ratio: Calculated by subtracting inventory from current assets, and then dividing by current liabilities. Another name for the quick ratio.

Acquiring firm: The firm that is buying another firm in a merger or acquisition.

Amortization schedule: Schedule that shows how a loan will be paid off by specifying both the principal and interest payments made per payment. Typically, the size of the payment is constant, but with each successive payment more goes to principal and less to interest.

Annual report: Report issued to stockholders by corporations that contains financial statements as well as management's opinion of the past year's operations and prospects for the future.

Bad debt: Situation that occurs when a seller extends credit to a buyer, and the buyer fails to pay the account.

Balance sheet: Basic accounting statement that records the assets of the firm and claims against them (liabilities and equities) at a specific instant in time.

Bankruptcy cost: Includes the direct legal costs and other opportunity costs, such as lost sales, bypassed capital budgeting projects, and the like, which investors cannot avoid by diversifying.

Bond: A long-term promissory note issued by the borrower promising to pay a specified interest per year and/or maturity value.

Book value: Assets minus liabilities, or stockholders' equity.

Book value per share: Stockholders' equity divided by the number of shares of common stock outstanding.

Capital budget: A statement of the firm's planned long-term investment projects, usually done annually.

Capital market: Financial market where long-term (greater than one year) financial assets such as bonds, preferred stock, or common stock are bought or sold.

Capital structure: The long-term financing of the firm, typically represented by long-term debt, leases, preferred stock, and common stock.

Cash budget: A detailed forecast of all expected cash inflows and outflows by the firm for some period of time.

Cash dividend (dividend):   The distribution to investors who own common or pre-ferred stock of some of the earnings of the firm.

Cash flow: The actual dollars coming into a firm (case inflow) or paid out by a firm (cash outflow).

Current ratio: Current assets divided by current liabilities; a measure of liquidity.

Debt: A loan made by a supplier of funds (creditor) to a demander of funds (debtor).

Depreciation: For accounting purposes, a charge against current income to record a portion of the historical cost of an asset.

Earnings after taxes (EAT):   Calculated by subtracting cost of goods sold, general and administrative expenses, depreciation, interest, and taxes from sales. Also called net income.

Factoring: The sale of a firm's accounts receivable as a means of spending up the inflow of funds, or to obtain a loan.

Financial intermediaries: Financial institutions such as banks, savings and loan associations, insurance companies, pension funds, and investment companies that assist in the transfer of funds from suppliers to demanders of these funds.

Financial leverage: The use of securities bearing a fixed (limited) charge to finance a portion of the firm's assets in order to increase the expected rate of return to common stockholders.

Financial plan: Plan based on cash flow projections that specifies where the firm is going and how it expects to get there.

Gross margin: Net sales minus cost of goods sold.

Gross profit margin: Gross margin divided by net sales; the percentage of each dollar of sales remaining after the cost of goods sold is taken into account.

Income statement: Basic accounting statement that records the results of the firm's operations over some period of time, typically a year. Indicates revenues, ex-penses, and resulting net income (or loss) for the firm.

Inventory turnover: Cost of goods sold divided by inventory. A ratio that mea-sures how many times a year the firm's inventory is turned over, or sold and replaced.

Leveraged buyout: A method whereby the buyer is allowed to use the assets of the venture as collateral for obtaining the funds necessary to purchase the en-trepreneur's venture.

Line of credit: Agreement between a company and a bank whereby the company can borrow up to a maximum amount.

Merger: The acquisition of a firm, a division of a firm, or part or all of its assets by another firm.

Net present value (NPV):   The present value of the future cash flows, discounted at the required rate of return (marginal cost of capital or risk-adjusted discount rate) minus the initial investment for the project.

Operating loss: A loss that occurs when a firm has negative taxable income (earn-ings before taxes).

Operating profit: Net sales minus all expenses except interest and taxes, but be-fore any adjustments.

Opportunity cost: The cost associated with an alternative or foregone opportunity that a firm or individual bypassed in order to accept another alternative.

Organized security exchanges: Formal organizations that have a physical location and exist to bring together buyers and sellers of securities in the secondary market.

Over-the-counter (OTC) market: A market for securities using telecommunications to bring together buyers and sellers of securities; a part of the secondary market.

Payback period: The amount of time (in years) for the expected cash inflows from a project to just equal the initial investment (or outflow) at time $t = 0$.

Preferred stock: Stock that has a prior, but generally limited, claim on assets and income before common stock, but after debt.

Present value (PV): The value today of a given future lump sum, or series of receipts, when discounted at a given discount rate.

Price earnings (P/E) ratio: Market price per share of common stock divided by earnings per share; shows how much investors are paying for one dollar of current earnings.

Prime rate: The rate charged the bank's best customers.

Principal: The amount of money that must be repaid by a borrower. Interest is figured on the principal.

Private placement: Financing directly between a demander and supplier of funds that bypasses the public and the underwriter.

Pro-forma financial statements: Forecasted financial statements; typically an income statement and a balance sheet, but could include a statement of changes in financial position.

Quick ratio: Current assets minus inventory divided by current liabilities—a measure of liquidity. Also called the acid test ratio.

Rate of return: The return earned on an investment. The expected rate of return is what is expected to be earned.

Required rate of return: The minimum rate of return necessary to attract an investor to purchase or continue to hold a security.

Retained earnings: An equity account on the balance sheet that reflects the sum of the firm's net income (losses) over its life, less all cash dividends paid.

Return on equity: Net income divided by stockholders' equity; or, return on total assets divided by one minus the total debt to the total debt to total asset ratio.

Return on total assets: Net income divided by total assets; or, net profit margin times total asset turnover. A profitability ratio that shows how much net income the firm generates per dollar of total assets. Often called return on investment (ROI).

Sales and leaseback: An arrangement arising when a firm sells an asset to another and simultaneously agrees to lease the property back for a specified number of years.

Term loan: Loans with maturities of one to ten years that are paid off by periodic payments over the life of the loan. Generally the payment is fixed at a given dollar amount per period, with more going to pay interest in the early payments and more to pay principal in the late payments.

Total debt to total assets: A ratio that indicates how much of the firm's funds are being supplied by its creditors.

About the Authors

Robert D. Hisrich is the Bovaird Chair Professor of Entrepreneurial Studies and Private Enterprise and professor of marketing at The University of Tulsa and is also president of H & P Associates, a marketing and management consulting firm he founded. He has previously served on the faculties of Boston College, Massachusetts Institute of Technology, National Institute for Higher Education (Ireland), and the University of Puerto Rico. Dr. Hisrich holds degrees from DePauw University and the University of Cincinnati. He spent several years in line and staff positions at Procter and Gamble and Ford Motor Company. While at Boston College, Dr. Hisrich ran the Small Business Institute, frequently winning the award for the best project in the state and region. He also was instrumental in establishing the Student Agency (a student entrepreneurial corporation) and the Small Business Development Center at the University. He is the author of four books: *Marketing a New Product: Its Planning, Development, and Management; The MBA Center; Marketing Decisions for New and Mature Products;* and *Marketing: A Practical Managerial Approach.* Dr. Hisrich has consulted to numerous large and small corporations, founded and operated several successful businesses, and designed and delivered management and entrepreneurial programs to U.S. and foreign businesses and governments.

Candida G. Brush received a Bachelor of Arts degree at the University of Colorado in Spanish and Latin American Studies. She did graduate work at Simmons College in Boston and Boston College, where she received a Master's in Business Administration and was awarded the Dean's Letter of Commendation for Special Achievement in working with the Small Business Development Center. Ms. Brush is presently a marketing instructor at Boston College and also teaches marketing-related courses in the Continuing Education Division of Cape Cod Community College. Her other endeavors include a consulting business specializing in consulting to entrepreneurs. Articles by Ms. Brush have been published in the *Journal of Small Business Management* and the *Proceedings of the 1982 Conference on Entrepreneurship*. She is continuing major research on many aspects of entrepreneurship.